THE LEADER UNWRITTEN

BECOMING WHO YOU'RE MEANT TO BE

PREMILA JINA

Copyright © Premila Jina
ISBN: 978-1-7641712-0-5

Dedication

To my husband and my two daughters—
I couldn't have done this without your love and support.
You are my strength, my inspiration, and my greatest joy.

Prologue

I didn't set out to write a book. I set out to survive.

If you've ever felt like you were navigating a world that wasn't built for you—starting over in a new place, a new career, or inside your own skin—you know that sometimes, thriving is a luxury. Some seasons are about keeping your head above water, finding small pockets of hope, and rewriting the story as you go. You do what you must to make it through, and then—maybe, if you're lucky—you look back and realize you've stitched together something like a life. Maybe not the life you planned, but a life that is yours.

So, no, this isn't a blueprint. It's not a list of hacks or clever shortcuts. What you're holding is a collection of lessons I learned the hard way—about hope, rest, reinvention, saying no, and all the other "soft" skills that aren't really soft at all. Most of the time, they're the only things that matter. This is a book about pivots and plot twists, about stories we outgrow and the quiet revolutions that happen when we choose ourselves, sometimes for the very first time.

Wherever you are—starting over, stuck in the middle, or just tired of pretending—I hope you find something here that feels like the beginning of your own next chapter.

The Battle Within: Two Wolves

As I write this, something ancient and deeply personal stirs inside me—a battle that's shaped every word, every chapter, every moment of this book.

There's a story I heard once, about two wolves within each of us. One wolf is shame. The other is wisdom. The one that wins is the one you feed.

The wolf of shame is relentless. It keeps a running commentary in my mind, whispering that I am not enough. That I am weak, imperfect, to blame for everything bad that's happened to me. Shame tells me that my low self-esteem and anger brought suffering upon myself, that my pain is a mark of my own failure. This wolf wants me to shrink, to play small, to disappear. It wraps me in guilt and humiliation, and tells me it would be safer if I just stayed silent.

But there's another voice, wisdom wolf. This one is fed every time someone reaches out, quietly, to say they see themselves in my story. When I share a post, and someone messages to say my vulnerability cracked something open for them. When a stranger admits, in a one-on-one conversation, that my words gave them the language for something they've never said out loud. This wolf is fed by connection, by purpose, by the possibility that my story might matter to someone else. I feel it grow stronger every time I hold space for someone else's truth—no judgment, just listening, just recognition. In these moments, I realize that what shames me most deeply is often what connects me to others most powerfully.

I didn't reach this place alone. I have sought therapy—sometimes in desperation, sometimes in hope. It's part of my journey, and I'm not ashamed to say so. But I've also discovered that telling my story, naming my shame, and making space for others to do the same is its own kind of therapy. This book is meant to be a workbook, a place for shared reflection, not just passive reading. My wish is that you'll engage with it: read, reflect, wrestle with the workbook questions. Let it be a companion as you harvest your own insights, make sense of your own story, and maybe, just maybe, find a little freedom.

The Silencing Power of Shame

I've always admired the courage of white women who stand on stages and tell the gritty, unvarnished truth of their lives. I've been awed by the power and presence of Black women who command a platform, their stories landing with the weight and dignity of survival and hard-won wisdom. But I almost never see brown, Indian women—women who look like me—stand up and tell their story, raw and real.

For years, I believed I would be that person. I told myself I would be the one to rip off the mask and say what no one else would. But as I sit here, even now, the wolf of shame whispers: You'll seem weak. You'll be boring. You'll be too factual. Don't embarrass yourself. Don't embarrass your family. It's a strange paradox. India is the land of Bollywood—drama, emotion, spectacle. But off-screen, our culture prizes the opposite: don't air your dirty laundry, don't be vulnerable, don't let anyone see your cracks. Curate your narrative. Project perfection.

I think a lot about this contradiction. The same society that creates films overflowing with song, tears, and confession, tells its daughters to keep quiet, to never bring shame to the family, to never show the world the messiness that lives inside every human life. The fear of being seen as imperfect is a powerful silencer.

I once watched a leader I deeply admire—a woman of Indian heritage—on stage. She told part of her story, and I caught, just for a moment, her hesitation. I recognized the tremor in her voice, the calculation in her eyes as she weighed each word. Would she be judged, misunderstood, labelled? I knew she was wrestling with the same cultural conditioning, the same fear of exposure and judgment, that I feel every time I share my story.

And yet, here I am, feeding the other wolf. Because I know what it feels like to listen from the shadows, to crave just one voice that sounds like mine, to need proof that I am not alone.

Why Stories Matter—And Why They're Hard to Tell

Why is it so hard for women like me to tell our stories? I think it's because we are raised to believe that perfection is not just expected, but required. Speak perfectly. Look perfect. Live a perfect life. Show only what is acceptable. Never, ever let on that you're struggling, or sad, or angry. Never make the family look bad. The risk isn't just personal—it's communal, generational. One woman's public "failure" reflects on the whole family, the whole community.

That's a lot to carry. It's no wonder the wolf of shame is so loud, so persistent.

But here's the thing: shame only survives in silence. The moment we name it, the moment we share our story with someone who can hold it gently, it starts to lose its power. I have learned this again and again, in hundreds of small conversations, some public, most private. When I risk vulnerability, I am almost always met with relief—someone else saying, "Me too," or "I thought I was the only one," or, "Thank you for putting words to what I've felt my whole life."

This is why I write. Not because I think my story is extraordinary, but because I know it's not. Because I know there are millions of us—women, minorities, anyone who has ever lived with the weight of being "other"—who have been told to keep quiet. Who have learned to survive by pretending. Who long to be seen and heard, just as we are.

The Purpose That Outlasts Fear

It would be a lie to say I'm not scared to write this book. I am. I worry about being misunderstood, about being judged, about bringing trouble to my family. I worry about being too much, or not enough. That's the wolf of shame, and it's never going away completely.

But the wolf of wisdom - purpose, of connection, of hope—that one gets stronger every day I choose to feed it. Because I know, deep down, that if my story can spark even a 1% shift in someone else's life—if it can offer a glimmer of hope, a moment of comfort, the relief of feeling less alone—then it's worth every ounce of fear. My aim is simple: to make a difference through my lived experience, to share the wisdom I've gained not in spite of my struggle, but because of it.

I am a lifelong learner. Books and stories have changed the course of my life more times than I can count. If this book, born from wrestling with my own two wolves, can help change the trajectory of yours—even by a fraction—then every word will have been worth it.

How to Use This Book

This book is a blend of memoir and workbook, designed for your active engagement. It is not a story to be read in one sitting. Instead, I invite you to treat it as a personal space for reflection. Pause after each chapter. Wrestle with the questions. Let yourself be uncomfortable, and above all, be honest. The work you do here is for you. Feel free to write in the margins, scribble your breakthroughs, and make this space your own.

The chapters are not chronological, because life rarely is. They are built around the themes that have **shaped my experience as a woman of colour**—challenges, lessons, and moments of clarity. **Each one is a story from my life, offered as a mirror for your own.**

My Journey: A 10,000-Foot View

To give you context for the stories ahead, here is the simple outline of my path. These are the guideposts that inform the perspective in this book:

My journey began in **India**, where I was born, before my family migrated to **Kenya** when I was four. For university, I moved to **London**, a city I would call home for eighteen years, building a career in the demanding world of investment banking and starting my own family. During this time, I also gained international experience through internships in **Switzerland**.

Seeking a different pace of life for my two children, I moved to **Australia**, and **Perth** is now where I live and work. This global path—across continents, cultures, and industries—has shaped every story and lesson within these pages.

Pearls of Insight

- ❖ **Shame as a Silencer:** The fear of shame, judgment, and bringing dishonour to one's family or community can be a powerful inhibitor of authentic self-expression and vulnerable storytelling.
- ❖ **Vulnerability Fosters Connection:** Sharing personal struggles and vulnerabilities, while daunting, can create deep connections with others who have similar experiences, helping them feel seen and less alone.
- ❖ **Representation Matters in Storytelling:** Seeing individuals from one's own cultural background share their authentic stories publicly can be incredibly empowering and can challenge ingrained cultural norms about silence and perfection.
- ❖ **Purpose Overcomes Fear:** A strong sense of purpose—such as wanting to help others or make a difference—can provide the courage needed to overcome the fear of shame and share one's story.

Your Turn: Reflect & Explore

1. **Your Two Wolves:** If you were to identify two internal "wolves" or conflicting voices that influence your willingness to be vulnerable or share your experiences, what would they be? What does each wolf typically whisper to you?

2. **The Fear of Judgment:** Think about a time you hesitated to share something personal or a vulnerable aspect of your story. What specific judgments or reactions were you most afraid of?
3. **The Power of Shared Story:** Can you recall a time when hearing someone else's vulnerable story made you feel understood, less alone, or inspired? What was it about their sharing that resonated with you? How might your own story, if shared, offer similar solace or inspiration to someone else?

If you take nothing else from this introduction, let it be this: you are not alone. The battle between shame and wisdom is universal. The courage to show up, to be seen, to speak the truth of your life, is a radical act. I hope this book helps you feed the wolf that leads you home to yourself.

PART I
ORIGINS & EARLY LESSONS

CHAPTER 1
Born in the Rann

The Rann of Kutch, India: a place where the earth cracks beneath your feet and the sky stretches into forever. Here, survival is a lesson learned before you can even speak its name. My story begins in this unforgiving landscape—a land that demanded resilience long before I understood what the word meant.

My earliest memories are not of the Rann itself, but of the stories told about it. My mother's voice, soft and steady, would paint pictures of dawns spent hauling water, of harvests snatched from the jaws of drought, of a life measured in small victories and quiet endurance. My grandmother's hands, rough and warm, would braid my hair and weave in the lessons of a land where nothing came easy.

Yet even as these stories took root in me, my own life was already in motion—pulled by forces much larger than I understood. My father, restless and ambitious, looked out at the horizon and saw only limits: caste, poverty, the snaking lines of debt that bound families to land. He wanted more, not just for himself, but for the family he and my mother were starting. While my mother was pregnant with me, he made the hardest decision of his life—he left the Rann behind and set out for Kenya.

I was born into absence and hope. My father was a distant voice in letters. My mother was both anchor and sail—steadying herself for the wait, carrying me and my older sister through the days with routines and rituals that stitched old world and new together. She would tell me, later, about the ache of that separation: the loneliness, the fear, and the stubborn pride that kept her moving forward.

In those early years, I was not the bright student people sometimes expect from stories like mine. School was confusing, overwhelming, a maze of unfamiliar rules. My sister seemed to glide through it, but I struggled—words twisted on the page, numbers refused to behave. The teachers, overworked and under-resourced, gave their attention to the shining stars. I was not one of them. I learned early how to disappear at the back of the classroom, how to turn shame into silence.

But home was different. My mother refused to let me shrink. Even as she managed the household and waited for news from my father, she made time to sit with me. She would not allow me to believe that I was less, that I was destined to stay behind. My sister, older and already shouldering responsibility, would sometimes help too—her patience a quiet gift. The three of us, together, became a small circle of resilience.

When I was four, our world shifted again. My mother made the decision to join my father in Kenya, packing up what little we had and setting out across continents. I remember the journey in fragments: the chaos of leaving, the tight grip of my mother's hand, my sister's calm beside me. Arrival was a shock—the air thick and new, the streets noisy, the taste of uncertainty in everything. We were outsiders, marked by our accents, our customs, our longing for a place that already felt like a story.

Kenya was not an easy home at first. The transition was rough, especially for a shy, struggling child. School here was different, the expectations unfamiliar. I was again the child who didn't quite fit, used to being behind, always playing catch-up. But my parents—now reunited—would not let me give up. My father, shaped by his own hard road, believed fiercely in the power of education. "No one can take away what you know," he would say, over and over, as if willing his faith into me.

My mother became the bridge between worlds: she kept the flavors and stories of the Rann alive in our home, even as she learned to navigate this new country. She modeled resilience not as stoicism, but as a commitment to keep moving, to keep hoping, to keep trying for something better. My sister became my secret guide—her example a light to follow, her encouragement a balm when I faltered.

Looking back, I see how migration, caste, and ambition were braided into every day of my childhood. I was raised on stories of what it meant to start with nothing, and on the unspoken challenge to make that "nothing" mean something. My earliest rebellion was not loud or dramatic. It was the stubborn refusal to believe that my starting point was my ending. Even when I struggled, even when I doubted, a tiny piece of me believed—because my mother, my father, and my sister believed first.

I learned early that where you begin shapes you, but it doesn't decide your ending. The lessons of the Rann, my family's courage, and the quiet rebellion of hope became the foundation for every new beginning. Wanting more was not shameful—it was our inheritance, our lifeline.

Pearls of Insight

- ❖ **Where You Start Isn't Where You Stay:** Your origins shape you, but they don't define your destination.
- ❖ **Resilience Is Braided, Not Born:** True strength is woven from the encouragement, sacrifice, and belief of those around you.
- ❖ **Invisible Struggles Matter:** The battles fought in silence often forge the deepest strength and empathy.

Your Turn: Reflect & Explore

1. **Mapping Your Beginnings:** What stories or lessons from your origins most shape how you face challenges today?
2. **Resilience Inventory:** Who helped you persist, and how do you carry their influence forward?
3. **Unseen Strengths:** Where did you develop your quietest strengths, and how might you honor them now?

As I crossed continents with my family, the lessons of the Rann traveled with me—quiet, persistent, and unyielding. But arriving in Kenya meant facing a new world of uncertainty, where I would have to discover what resilience and belonging looked like all over again.

CHAPTER 2
Stones and Sticks

What does it mean to be a stranger—small, uncertain, clutching your mother's hand in a place where even the sunlight feels foreign? My first memory of Kenya is the ache of not belonging, and the quiet determination to make a home out of whatever we could find.

When I think back to my first years in Kenya, I remember the sharp edges of adaptation. We arrived in Nakuru as outsiders, carrying more hope than certainty. The air was different, the rhythms unfamiliar; even the light seemed to fall differently on our skin. There was the faint, persistent ache of homesickness—for the Rann, for the only reality I had known, for the father who was still learning to be a father in a new world. I was four years old, trailing behind my mother and older sister, learning to build a life from scratch with little more than resourcefulness and the quiet determination not to be left behind.

We landed in a town that, to my young mind, felt like a single street suspended between the gentle chaos of the market and the industrial area. The main street—Kenyatta Avenue, though I was too young to know its name—was the town's spine. Everything important seemed to happen along this stretch: mothers bargaining for vegetables, men in dust-streaked cloths hurrying to open shops, children dashing from school to home. Beyond it, the world faded into quieter neighborhoods and, eventually, the wild expanse of the lake, rimmed by flamingos so bright they seemed almost unreal.

The Kenya of the early 1980s was a place in transition, still carving out its identity in the aftermath of independence. For a newly arrived immigrant family, it was a place of both promise and uncertainty. My mother, my sister, and I clung to each other, learning to navigate a language we didn't yet speak, customs we didn't yet understand, and the constant sense of being observed—marked as different, as new.

Resourcefulness became our superpower. My mother was a master of making something out of nothing. She could transform a sparse pantry into a meal that tasted like home, patch a torn dress so cleverly you'd never see the seams, wrangle a day's worth of errands with a smile. She taught my sister and me that lack did not mean limitation—it was just another kind of challenge, a puzzle to be solved. In those early days, adaptation didn't mean losing ourselves or forgetting where we came from; it meant learning to belong in new ways, to build bridges out of stones and sticks.

School, again, was a battleground. The language of instruction was English, but the playground spoke Swahili, and I spoke a hybrid mix of Gujarati and the hesitant words I picked up from context and repetition. I was still not the star student, still haunted by the feeling of always playing catch-up. My sister, older and already accustomed to the role of protector, helped me decode homework and navigate the social hierarchies. Our teachers were a mixed bag—some kind, some indifferent, a few who saw my struggle and offered encouragement, most who simply moved on to the next hand raised.

In the midst of all this, I learned that leadership sometimes means noticing who is left out and making space for them. I remember, even as a child, gravitating toward the girl sitting alone at lunch, the boy who always seemed lost at recess. Maybe I recognized in them the same uncertainty I felt. Maybe I was just looking for a friend. But that impulse—to include, to gather, to build something out of what others overlooked—became a quiet thread running through my life.

Our connection to the wider world was rationed, measured in small doses. We had a boxy black-and-white television that flickered to life in the late afternoons and went dark again by nine. The programming was mostly in Swahili, with the occasional English show—a fragment of news, a cartoon, a dubbed soap opera. It was a window, but a narrow one. Sometimes, watching the screen, I felt as if the world ended at the edges of our town, that there was nothing beyond the Rift Valley hills but more hills, more sky, more of the same.

But even as my world felt small, my imagination rebelled. If the television was a window, books were a door flung wide open. Saturday evenings were sacred: the trip to the local library, a private one run by the Indian community, was the highlight of my week. The moment I stepped inside, Nakuru's boundaries dissolved. I could be anyone, go anywhere. The cobbled lanes of Enid Blyton's England, the secretive woods of the Famous Five, the clue-strewn mansions of Nancy Drew—these became as familiar to me as the dusty roads outside our house. I learned to see myself as a detective, an adventurer, a girl who could solve mysteries and cross oceans, even if only in my mind.

My greatest treasure, though, was Reader's Digest. I devoured every issue I could get my hands on, cover to cover. The articles were a lifeline: stories of survival, breakthroughs, humor, and hope, all condensed into a magazine that seemed, to me, to contain the whole world. I learned new words, new places, new ways of seeing. Each story chipped away at my childish certainty that the world was flat, that nothing existed beyond what I could see or touch. The world grew larger, richer, more complex with every page I turned.

There was also the ritual of the Sunday newspaper. My father would buy it, and the moment he walked in the door, a friendly scuffle would break out among us. My sister went straight for the news and the editorials, I went for the comics, the puzzles, then the news. Even when I didn't understand everything, I loved the feeling of being let in on important conversations, the sense that

I was eavesdropping on the adult world. It fed my curiosity and, slowly, my confidence.

Reading was more than a pastime; it was a quiet act of rebellion. In a world that seemed intent on telling me where my boundaries were, books and magazines showed me how to redraw them. My hunger to know—to discover, to connect, to understand—became the engine that powered me through the awkward years of adaptation. I began to realize that resourcefulness wasn't just about patching clothes or stretching a meal. It was a kind of wealth, a way of moving through the world that valued creativity over conformity, possibility over resignation.

Nakuru, with its single street and infinite worlds within, taught me to see beyond what was given. My friends and I invented games with whatever we could find—stones and sticks, bottle caps, scraps of cloth. We built entire universes in the spaces between chores and homework. The town might have felt contained, but our imaginations were boundless. I learned that limits are often more imagined than real, that the ability to adapt is a form of quiet power.

That hunger for more, for elsewhere, never really left me. Today, it shows up as a restless curiosity—a need to read, to listen, to learn, to connect ideas across continents and cultures. I still devour books, articles, podcasts, anything that feeds the fire. It's no longer about escape, but about understanding. The question has shifted from "What's out there?" to "How does it work, and how can I use it?" The little girl lost in the library learned to navigate the real world with the same sense of wonder and possibility she once reserved for fiction.

Adaptation, I've learned, isn't about losing yourself. It's about discovering new ways to belong, about building bridges out of whatever materials you have on hand—stones, sticks, books, questions. It's about finding the others who feel left out and making space for them at your table. It's about turning scarcity into abundance, not by denying what's missing, but by multiplying what you already have.

Nakuru taught me that adaptation is not about erasing yourself, but about building bridges—sometimes out of nothing more than stones, sticks, and stubborn hope. Every act of curiosity, every new word learned, was a step toward belonging and a quiet act of leadership.

Pearls of Insight

- **Adaptation isn't about losing yourself; it's about learning how to belong in new ways.**
- **Resourcefulness is a kind of wealth.**
- **Curiosity as a Compass:** Even in environments with perceived limitations, innate curiosity can guide you to find windows to vastly larger worlds.
- **Reading is Rebellion:** Choosing to read widely and deeply can be a quiet act of rebellion against intellectual or geographical constraints, empowering you to define your own horizons.
- **Knowledge Builds Bridges:** Every piece of information absorbed, every story read, builds a bridge from your personal experience to the universal human experience, fostering empathy and understanding.
- **Lifelong Learning Starts Young:** The seeds of intellectual hunger planted in childhood through simple acts like reading can blossom into a lifelong pursuit of knowledge, adaptation, and growth.

Reflect & Explore

1. **What Were Your Windows?** Growing up, what were your "windows" to the wider world beyond your immediate family or town? (e.g., books, music, a specific person, travel, TV). How did they shape your understanding or aspirations?
2. **Feeding Your Curiosity Now:** How do you intentionally feed your curiosity today? Where do you go (physically or digitally) to learn new things just for the sake of knowing or understanding?
3. **Beyond Limitations:** Think of a current situation where you feel limited or constrained (perhaps in your career, community, or personal growth). How could you apply the principle of "reading your way out"—actively seeking knowledge, perspectives, or skills—to expand your possibilities within that situation?

As I learned to belong in Nakuru, my hunger for understanding grew—each new word, each new friend, a small rebellion against the boundaries of my world. But soon, I would be tested in ways that would demand not just adaptation, but the courage to stand up and speak out.

CHAPTER 3
From Victim to Perpetrator, and the Long Shadow of the Playground

What if the playground, a place meant for laughter, is where we first learn the harsh lessons of power and pain? My journey from victim to perpetrator began here, in the shadows of childhood games that taught me about cruelty, survival, and the long shadows they cast into adulthood.

The playground is supposed to be a place of laughter and scraped knees, of friendships and games that spill into the rest of your childhood. But for many of us, it's also the first place we truly encounter cruelty—the first venue where the complex machinery of power, inclusion, and exclusion starts to grind away at our sense of self. It's where we learn, painfully, that pain doesn't just sit quietly inside us; left unchecked, it ricochets outward, seeking release. And sometimes, in our desperation not to be hurt, we become the ones who hurt others.

This is the story of how I learned that lesson the hard way, and how its shadow followed me well into adulthood.

The Birth of a Bully

It started, as these things often do, with something small. I was in primary school in Kenya, a brown girl among a sea of faces, some like mine, some not. There was a girl named Angi, a black girl, who lived along my route to school. At first, she seemed just another member of the crowd, but soon she began to stand out in the most painful way. She'd wait for me, join our little walking group, and, out of sight of the others, begin her torment: sharp pinches to my arm, whispered threats, the demand for my treasured mabuyu—those sweet-tangy Kenyan snacks I loved. She'd make me buy them for her, and if I didn't, there would be consequences.

It was never just Angi for long. Her group grew—four girls, all with their own silent wounds, all hungry for a taste of control in a world that kept snatching it away from them. My daily walk to school became a gauntlet; breaktimes and class changes, minefields of anxiety. They took whatever little nice thing I had, and I learned to keep my head down, to move quietly, to hope for invisibility.

Looking back, I realize even then I had some awareness of Angi's pain. There were rumors about her broken home, a father who'd run off, a mother struggling to hold things together, a harsh grandmother who ruled with an iron fist. I could see the ache in her eyes, the brittleness in her anger. But that didn't make her pinches hurt any less.

The Shift: When Victims Join the Pack

Eventually, the dynamic changed—although not in the way I would have chosen. One day, Angi and her friends told me to join them in chasing a boy home. I did. And just like that, I was no longer the prey. I'd crossed the invisible line from victim to participant, and the bullying I'd suffered abruptly stopped.

The relief was overwhelming. For the first time, I wasn't dreading the walk to school. For the first time, I felt—if not powerful, then at least safe. The price for that safety was simple: I had to do to others what had been done to me. We chased boys home, snatched snacks from other kids, built a new hierarchy that depended on someone always being on the bottom. The gang grew, absorbing other Indian girls who, just like me, had been on the outside and were desperate for any kind of reprieve.

It is a deeply human thing, I think, to want to belong. The playground teaches you quickly that inclusion—any inclusion—is better than isolation. I wish I could say I was wracked with guilt, but the truth is, at the time, my sense of relief was bigger than any pang of conscience.

The Power of Authority

The cycle finally broke when, inevitably, another child complained. The teachers got involved. I still remember the way they called us in, their voices stern and unyielding. In that moment, I saw something that stuck with me for years: even the most feared bullies were afraid of the teachers. Adult intervention, swift and certain, brought the whole charade to a halt.

In the aftermath, I realized something else. If authority could break the power of the bullies, maybe I needed to build alliances with authority figures, too. From then on, I made sure to stay close to teachers, to be noticed by them, to have them on my side. It was a child's simple logic, but it served me well—at least for a while.

Did I feel remorse for those I'd bullied? Maybe a flicker, but mostly I was just relieved to be done with my own pain. I told myself that I wasn't responsible for what happened to me—and by extension, I wasn't really responsible for what I did to others. This, I now realize, is how cycles of harm perpetuate themselves: pain passed down, justified, never properly addressed.

The Long Shadow: Bullying Grows Up

The playground may fade, but its lessons linger. Over the years, I've watched the same dynamics play out in boardrooms, offices, and group chats. The tactics get subtler, the stakes higher, but the core truth remains: pain unhealed gets passed on.

In the workplace, I've been on the receiving end of bullying and harassment more than once. Only now, the bullies wear suits and wield emails instead of pinches and whispered threats. They manipulate processes, weaponize policies, and hide behind "professionalism." The playground's crude power plays become office politics, exclusion from meetings, or being undermined in front of colleagues.

And unlike the teachers of my childhood, who stepped in and made the bullying stop, the adults in charge at work are often reluctant to intervene. HR can feel like a "cliquey girls' club," more concerned with protecting the organization than the individual. Managers, unwilling or unable to deal with conflict, tell you to "work it out yourselves." Your complaints are minimized: "You're too sensitive." "He's just having a rough time." "It's all in your head." Anti-bullying policies exist, but the processes for proving harm and getting justice are often so convoluted, so discouraging, that most people give up before they even start.

It's the same story, just with bigger consequences.

Survival Strategies

So how do we cope? We build new protective mechanisms. We seek out powerful allies, hope for a leader with integrity, document every slight and slight every document, just in case. Some of us master the art of blending in, never drawing attention to ourselves. Others become hyper-vigilant, always on the lookout for threats. Some turn cynical, assuming the worst of everyone.

And some—just like on the playground—become bullies themselves. The cycle continues, dressed up in adult clothes, but driven by the same old wounds.

The Cost of Unhealed Pain

Looking back, I can see how desperately I wanted to avoid pain—how I'd do almost anything to keep from being the one left out, the one targeted. It's a familiar story for anyone who's ever lived on the margins: the hunger for safety, the longing for acceptance, the willingness to do things you're not proud of just to belong.

But the relief is never complete. The guilt lingers, the shame festers. And until we find the courage to confront the pain at its source—to name it, to feel it, to forgive ourselves and make amends—it keeps finding new ways to spill out into the world.

It took me years to fully reckon with my part in that playground drama. For a long time, I justified it—told myself I was just a kid, that I didn't know better, that my own suffering excused my actions. But deep down, I knew the truth: pain that isn't healed gets passed on. The only way to break the cycle is to take responsibility, to make amends, to forgive ourselves and those who hurt us.

The Role of Remorse and Accountability

True strength, I've learned, isn't about power or control. It's about accountability. It's about looking back at the ways you've hurt others—intentionally or not—and having the courage to say, "I'm sorry." It's about making amends, not because you want to feel better (though you will), but because it's the right thing to do.

I've tried, as an adult, to find the people I hurt and apologize. Sometimes it's possible; sometimes it's not. Sometimes the best you can do is to live differently, to break the cycle in your own life, to make sure you never put anyone else through what you went through.

And it's about forgiving yourself, too. Shame wants us to believe we're irredeemable, that our worst moments define us forever. But healing means making peace with the past—not erasing it, but learning from it, growing through it, and using that growth to help others.

The Cycle in the Next Generation

One thing I deeply value about the world my children are growing up in is the way schools now talk openly about bullying. From Year 1, they are taught about empathy, about the emotional impact of cruelty, about the ways in which hurt people hurt people. There are chaplains, counselors, support workers—adults whose job it is to help kids process their pain before it festers into something toxic.

I see the difference it makes. My kids' school is not perfect—no school is—but there's an awareness, a willingness to intervene, that simply didn't exist in my day. The hope, of course, is that if we can catch these patterns early, if we can teach children to name their pain and ask for help, we can prevent the cycle from taking root.

Breaking the Cycle as Adults

But what about us, the adults who grew up before these conversations were normal? We carry our unhealed wounds into every boardroom, every friendship, every family dinner. We have to do the work ourselves—to unlearn the lessons of the playground, to build new ways of relating, to create spaces where pain can be named and healed instead of hidden and passed on.

That starts with honesty. With looking at our own behavior, our own complicity, our own pain. With seeking help when we need it, and offering help when we can. With refusing to minimize or excuse harm, no matter who it comes from or how it's dressed up.

It means holding each other accountable, not just for the harm we cause but for the harm we allow to continue. It means refusing to be bystanders—on the playground, in the office, at home.

And it means building systems—at work, at school, in our communities—that make it easier to speak up, to get help, to find justice. Authority, when wielded with integrity, is a powerful force for good. But it's up to us to demand that from our leaders, and to be those leaders when we can.

Healing starts with owning our stories—acknowledging the pain we've endured and the harm we've caused. Only then can we break the cycle, build new ways of relating, and create a world where empathy and accountability lead the way.

Pearls of Insight

- ❖ **Bullying is a Cycle:** Victims often become perpetrators, seeking relief from their own pain by inflicting it on others. Breaking this cycle requires courage and self-awareness.
- ❖ **Underlying Pain Fuels Aggression:** The root of bullying is almost always unaddressed pain or trauma. Compassion for the bully does not excuse their behavior, but it does point to where healing must begin.
- ❖ **The Power of Authority and Intervention:** Decisive action from those in power—teachers, managers, leaders—can disrupt cycles of harm and create space for healing.
- ❖ **Workplace Bullying Mimics Playground Tactics:** The behaviors don't change, they just get more sophisticated. Adult bullies use policies and procedures to hide their aggression.

- ❖ **Invalidation Perpetuates Harm:** When people's experiences are dismissed or minimized, the harm deepens and the cycle continues.
- ❖ **Proactive Education is Key:** Teaching empathy, conflict resolution, and emotional literacy from a young age is crucial.
- ❖ **Support for Both Victim and Aggressor:** Healing the underlying pain of the bully, as well as supporting the victim, is the only way to truly break the cycle.

Reflect & Explore

1. **Playground Echoes:** Reflect on your own early school experiences. Did you witness or experience bullying? How did those early dynamics of power, inclusion, and exclusion shape your understanding of social interactions?
2. **Workplace Dynamics:** Have you ever witnessed or experienced behaviors in a workplace that felt like adult bullying or microaggressions, even if not explicitly labeled as such? How did the environment or leadership respond?
3. **Creating Safe Spaces:** What is one concrete action you can take, in your current sphere of influence (as a parent, colleague, leader, or friend), to help create a safer, more supportive environment where individuals feel empowered to speak up against unfair treatment and where those in pain are offered support rather than resorting to aggression?

The lessons of the playground didn't end with childhood. As I grew, I saw those same dynamics play out in new arenas, challenging me to confront pain, seek healing, and lead with integrity.

CHAPTER 4
Feet in Two Worlds, But Belong Nowhere

What happens when the home your parents remember no longer exists—and the world outside your door doesn't quite let you in? My childhood in Kenya was shaped by the fierce preservation of an imagined India, a place built from memories, rituals, and rules that didn't always fit the world we lived in. I grew up learning to navigate the space between two cultures, always searching for a place to belong.

The Notion of India: Childhood in Kenya

My earliest memories are not of the land where I was born, but of a place where my family tried to recreate it. My parents migrated to Kenya when we were very young—my father had moved four years before the rest of us, laying the groundwork for a new life in a foreign land. Yet, in our home in Nakuru, a small Kenyan town, it felt as if we had never left India. My parents clung fiercely to their idea of India, an idea shaped by the values and traditions of Gandhi's days. Their India was one of strict codes: no sleeveless clothes, no revealing outfits, hair always neatly plated, and impeccable manners. Everyone was "uncle" or "aunty," and any deviation—smoking, drinking, clubbing—was branded as rebellion. Meat was out of the question.

We lived in a close-knit Indian community, a bubble of shared nostalgia and inherited customs. Our festivals were celebrated with the same fervor as in the old country, our language and rituals carefully preserved. For my parents, this was safety—a way to anchor themselves in a world that felt otherwise unpredictable and foreign.

A Shocking Encounter with Modern India

At fifteen, I traveled to India with my sister and cousin brother. I expected to find the India my parents spoke of, but what I found in Ahmedabad was a revelation. The girls there wore clothes my mother would never have allowed. They spoke their minds, studied at university, rode motorbikes, and some even had relationships before marriage. They danced with abandon, went out for late-night movies, and clubbing was normal. These women were free in ways I had never imagined.

I was confused. This version of India did not fit the narrative I had grown up with. I realized, of course, that Ahmedabad was a city, not a remote village in Kutch, but the contrast was stark. When I tried to tell my parents about this other India, they refused to listen. Even when they visited the city, they saw only what fit their version of India, dragging us to temples and villages. Years later, I would learn this was confirmation bias—the tendency to see only what supports your existing beliefs.

The Struggle for Progress

As an Indian in Kenya, progress was hard-won. My sister fought to do A-levels and go to college; I had to fight even harder to attend university. I was the first woman in my extended family to do so—a milestone. Yet, in the bustling cities of India, women were already earning master's degrees and building careers. What felt like breaking glass ceilings in Kenya was already the norm in urban India.

This is the invisible battle migrant children face. Our parents left India with a fixed notion of their homeland, and in a foreign country, where everything is uncertain, they built a community around that notion. It gave them comfort and a sense of belonging. For us, the next generation, it meant living with a foot in two worlds—Indian and Western—but belonging to neither.

The Invisible Battle: Identity and Belonging

When we visit India, we are seen as foreigners—sometimes even as more conservative or backward than the women in these cities. In Kenya, we are still outsiders. We try to ground ourselves in flowing water, always moving, never fully at rest.

I have always struggled with my identity. Born in India, but not fully Indian; brought up in Kenya, but not fully Kenyan; lived in London for eighteen years, but not fully British; now in Australia, but not fully Australian. I am an immigrant in every country, searching for a sense of belonging.

The Safety of Community, the Weight of Tradition

In Kenya, the Indian community was our safety net. We were a minority, and the community offered protection, familiarity, and shared values. But it also meant that change came slowly. Parents, clinging to their memories, enforced rules that felt outdated to us. The community reinforced these norms, and any attempt to break away was met with resistance.

Yet, outside the community, we were different. At school, our lunches smelled of spices, our clothes were sometimes "too traditional," and our customs misunderstood. We learned to code-switch—to be one person at home and another outside.

This duality was exhausting, and it bred a sense of not fully belonging anywhere.

The Cost of Being Between Worlds

As I grew older, the feeling of being split between worlds only intensified. In India, I was the foreign cousin, the one who didn't quite fit in. My accent was different, my manners too formal, my clothes too modest. In Kenya, I was Indian, but not Kenyan enough. In London, I was an immigrant, always aware of my difference. Now in Australia, I am still an outsider, even as I put down roots.

This is the migrant's paradox: we carry our parents' nostalgia, but we also see the world changing around us. We are expected to honor the past, but we are shaped by the present. We are told to fit in, but also to stand out. We are always negotiating, always adapting, always searching for home.

Learning to Embrace Difference

Over time, I have learned to see my difference as a strength. I love learning about other cultures, hearing people's stories, understanding their histories. I have grown roots in Australia, and this is now home. In Australia, everyone except the Aboriginal people is a migrant. I, too, am a migrant—one among many, each with our own story of belonging and not belonging.

The Unseen Strength of the In-Between

Living between worlds has taught me resilience, empathy, and adaptability. I have learned to navigate different cultures, to find common ground, to build bridges. I have learned that identity is not fixed, but fluid—a tapestry woven from many threads.

Yet, there are moments when the longing for belonging returns. When I hear a song from my childhood, smell a familiar spice, or see an old photograph, I am transported back to Nakuru, to the safety of my community, to the comfort of my parents' India. But I know that I can never truly return—not to that India, not to that Kenya, not even to the London I once called home.

Carving Out a New Future

For those of us with feet in two worlds, the task is not to choose one over the other, but to carve out a new space—a space where we can belong on our own terms. This means honoring our heritage, but also embracing change. It means challenging old norms, but also respecting the struggles of those who came before us. It means building new communities, forging new identities, and creating a future that is both rooted and open.

The Journey Continues

The journey of belonging is never complete. It is a process of negotiation, adaptation, and growth. It is about finding home—not in a place, but in ourselves. For me, that journey has taken me across continents and cultures, through moments of confusion and clarity, loss and discovery.

I am still learning what it means to belong. But I know now that I am not alone. There are many of us—children of migrants, citizens of the world, with feet in two worlds and hearts that belong everywhere and nowhere. Our stories are not of loss, but of possibility. We are the bridge between past and future, tradition and change. And in that, perhaps, we find our true belonging.

In the end, I've learned that true belonging isn't about choosing one world over another, but about carving out a space where all the pieces of who you are can coexist. My journey is far from over, but I now see that living between worlds is not just a challenge—it's a source of strength, resilience, and possibility.

Pearls of Insight: What I Have Learned

- ❖ **True belonging is not about fitting in**, but about being accepted for who you are, in all your complexity.
- ❖ **Identity is not a single story**, but a collection of experiences, memories, and hopes.
- ❖ **Carrying two cultures is a source of strength**, even when it feels like a burden.
- ❖ **Living your values is hard**, especially when the world around you does not reflect them—but it is the only way to build trust, within yourself and with others.
- ❖ **Community matters.** Finding or building a community of people who understand your journey can make all the difference.
- ❖ **Language is more than words;** it is a bridge to belonging, both to your roots and to your new home.
- ❖ **Home is not a place, but a feeling**—and sometimes, we must learn to carry that feeling within ourselves.

Your Turn: Reflect and Explore

1. **What are your core values?** How do you live them, even when it is hard?
2. **Where do you feel most at home?** What makes that place (or community) feel like home?
3. How do you navigate the tension between honoring your heritage and embracing your present?
4. What stories do you tell yourself about who you are, and how might those stories evolve?

As I continue to walk this path between cultures and continents, the next chapter of my story asks a deeper question: How do you build a life—and a sense of self—when the ground beneath you is always shifting?.

CHAPTER 5
The Colour of Confidence

Childhood Unawareness

When I was a toddler, I never thought about my skin tone. It simply wasn't something I noticed, much less worried about. My world was small—my family, our home, the local shops, the streets I played on. I attended a semi-government school for primary education, a place that straddled the line between public and private. It wasn't the rough-and-tumble government school my parents warned me about, but it wasn't the polished, exclusive realm of the private schools either. It was a jumble—a melting pot of children from all walks of life. There were Indian kids, African kids, and, as I remember it, two white children who seemed to float through the corridors with a kind of effortless grace. They were the recipients of a gentle, positive attention, admired but never envied, their difference a curiosity rather than a wedge.

It was there, amid the noise of the playground and the echo of lessons, that I first became aware of the colour of my skin. Not just that I was Indian, but that I was a particular kind of Indian—one whose skin was darker than most of my classmates. In the unspoken but rigid hierarchy of Indian society, skin tone was a currency, and mine, I quickly learned, was of the lowest denomination.

The Indian Spectrum

For an Indian girl, the spectrum of skin tones is not just a matter of genetics; it's a social ranking system. Bollywood, that great mirror and moulder of Indian ideals, had already set the rules: fair was beautiful, fair was intelligent, fair was desirable. The heroines were always pale, their skin glowing with an almost otherworldly light. The villains, the comic relief, the background extras—these roles were reserved for the darker-skinned. It was a message so pervasive, so insidious, that it seeped into every conversation, every compliment, every whispered warning from well-meaning aunties: "You're so dark, dear. You must do something about it if you want a good husband."

At school, my place on the spectrum was clear. In the Indian context, I was at the very end—darker than most, my skin a deep brown that marked me as different even among my own. But there were African children, too, whose skin was even darker. I watched them, curious. They seemed to own their colour with a kind of power, a pride that I admired but could not emulate. Did it matter to them, I wondered, the way it mattered to me? If it did, they never showed it.

Home Remedies and Hope

Growing up, I desperately wanted to be fair. I tried everything—homemade masks concocted from whatever I could find in the kitchen cupboard. Avocado, turmeric, yogurt, lemon juice. I'd smear these mixtures on my face, hopeful that when I washed them off, I'd see a lighter girl in the mirror. Sometimes my skin felt softer, sometimes it glowed, but it never changed colour. Still, I persisted, convinced that the right combination would unlock the secret to beauty.

To counter my growing obsession, I threw myself into sports. I played everything: netball, volleyball, football, hockey—any game that kept me outside, moving, alive. The sun became my companion, darkening my skin further, but I didn't care. On the field, my body was strong, my mind sharp, and for a few hours, I forgot about the colour of my skin.

But the questions lingered. I'd ask my parents, "Why are you fair and I'm not?" They'd laugh it off or change the subject, unwilling or unable to explain the genetic lottery that had left me feeling like an outsider in my own family.

The Industry of Fairness

As I grew older, the pressure only intensified. I became aware of an entire industry built on the promise of fairness. Creams, lotions, treatments—products with names like "Fair & Lovely" lined the shelves of every Indian store. I tried them all, slathering my face with chemicals that stung and burned, hoping for a miracle. Before weddings or big functions, I'd visit the hairdresser for a skin-bleaching treatment, enduring the discomfort for the promise of a lighter complexion.

I knew it wasn't good for my skin, but the desire to be beautiful—by the standards I'd been taught—overpowered my common sense. I was clever, excelling academically at that point, always at the top of my class. But in the eyes of my community, intelligence was secondary. Beauty, and by extension, fairness, came first.

The Weight of Words

The comments from relatives and family friends stung the most. "You're so dark, you won't find a nice boy to marry," they'd say, their voices dripping with concern. "You should do something about it." I hated my skin tone, hated the way it made me feel—less than, unworthy, invisible.

A New World: London

Everything changed when I moved to London. Suddenly, I was on another planet. My skin, once a source of shame, became an asset. My white friends spent small fortunes on tanning beds and bronzing products, desperate for the very colour I'd spent years trying to erase. It didn't make sense. How could something so undesirable in one place be so coveted in another?

During my internships in Switzerland, working for one of the largest banks, I dressed well, carried myself with confidence. People would stop me in the street, mistaking me for a Bollywood actress, asking for autographs. I was showered with attention, dates, gifts. I went from being invisible in Kenya's Indian community to being seen—really seen—in Europe.

The thing is, my skin colour hadn't changed. The environment had.

The Colonial Hangover

In the Indian community, the obsession with fairness is rooted in history. Colonisation left a deep scar, embedding the idea that fair skin meant power, intelligence, desirability. The British were the rulers, pale and untouchable, while the colonised were darker, their skin a mark of their subjugation. This belief persisted, passed down through generations, reinforced by media, family, and society.

But for the British and Europeans, the perception was entirely different. They longed for the "healthy-looking" brown glow that their own pale skin, starved of sunlight, could not provide. In their eyes, my skin was beautiful, exotic, desirable.

Confidence and Colour

My confidence was inextricably linked to my skin colour. In Kenya, I felt ugly, unworthy. In Switzerland, I felt beautiful, powerful. When I felt confident, I was more outgoing, more energetic, more willing to ask for what I wanted. I didn't need courage; I simply did things, feeling entitled, gifted, privileged. It was easy.

But when I felt ugly, everything required courage. Every action took energy, every word was a struggle. How could something as superficial as skin colour have such a profound impact on my sense of self? And yet, that was my lived experience.

The Power of Environment

Looking back, I realise that my journey was never really about my skin. It was about the power of environment, the weight of perception, the stories we tell ourselves and each other. In one place, I was invisible; in another, I was celebrated. The only thing that changed was the lens through which I was viewed.

Owning My Story

Today, I own my story. I own my skin, my history, my journey. I am proud of the girl who smeared avocado on her face, desperate to fit in. I am proud of the woman who walked the streets of London and Zurich, head held high, finally comfortable in her own skin.

I have learned that beauty is not a standard set by others, but a truth you claim for yourself. I have learned that confidence is not about meeting someone else's expectations, but about living your own values, every single day.

From Shame to Strength

There are still days when the old doubts creep in, when I hear the voices of those aunties in my head, warning me that I am too dark, too different. But I remind myself that my worth is not defined by the colour of my skin, but by the content of my character, the strength of my convictions, the courage to live my values in a world that often rewards conformity over authenticity.

I am more than the sum of my parts, more than the product of my environment. I am a work in progress, a living testament to the power of resilience, the importance of self-acceptance, and the enduring truth that we are all, in the end, the authors of our own stories.

The Colour of Confidence

My journey has taught me that confidence is not about the colour of your skin, but about the courage to live your truth. It's about choosing, every day, to show up as yourself, to own your story, to refuse to be defined by someone else's standards.

So to anyone who has ever felt less than, who has ever doubted their worth because of the way they look—know this: you are enough. Your value is not determined by the shade of your skin, but by the light you bring to the world.

Pearls of Insight: What I Have Learned

- ❖ My confidence and self-doubt were shaped by the world around me.
- ❖ As a child, I never questioned my skin tone until others pointed it out as different.
- ❖ Growing up in a society that prized fairness, I internalized the belief that lighter skin meant greater beauty, intelligence, and worth.
- ❖ I tried countless remedies to change my skin tone, chasing an ideal that was never truly in my control.
- ❖ My skin didn't change, only the way others saw it did— showing me that confidence is deeply tied to context.
- ❖ I learned that our sense of self can be diminished or uplifted by the perceptions of those around us.

❖ My worth is not determined by my skin colour, but by my character and my courage to be authentic—even when it's difficult.

Reflect & Explore

1. When did you first notice something about yourself that made you feel different, and how did it shape your self-image?
2. How have the places you've lived or the people around you influenced your confidence or sense of belonging?
3. What personal stories or beliefs are you ready to let go of so you can embrace your authentic self?

Live your values. Own your story. And remember—the only approval you need is your own

CHAPTER 6
Anger is not a flaw

What if everything you were taught about anger was a lie? As a girl, I learned to swallow my rage, to silence my voice, to trade honesty for acceptance. But beneath the surface, anger simmered—a signal that something was deeply wrong, not with me, but with the world that demanded my silence.

If you grow up as a girl in a world that values silence over honesty, you learn early to swallow your anger. I was told, over and over, "Don't be angry." The words came from every direction—family, teachers, aunties, uncles, neighbors, the society at large. For a while, I believed them. I thought maybe I was broken for feeling anger so fiercely, for letting it spill out of me, for refusing to stuff it down and play nice.

But here's the truth: anger was never my problem. The real problem was hypocrisy—the kind that runs deep in every community, every system, every so-called "refined" society.

I landed in Kenya as a wild, loud girl straight off a flight from India, and the contrast was immediate. Kenya's Indian community was close-knit, tightly wound, obsessed with appearances and rules. There was a script for how to behave, how to dress, how to speak, how to fit in. I didn't know the script, and even if I had, I'm not sure I could have followed it. I came from a family of farmers—low caste, already marked as outsiders. My sister and I were seen as wild brats, too loud, too unruly, too unwilling to bend.

My sister adapted quickly. She became eloquent, stylish, confident—the kind of girl who could walk into a room and silence it with her presence. People were in awe of her. She had the self-assurance that makes adults nervous. But I was different. Defiant. I saw the rules for what they were: a way to keep people in their place, to reward the compliant and punish the outliers. I saw the hypocrisy—adults who preached respect but gossiped and sniped and bullied behind closed doors. The same people who told us to be "cultured" let their own anger and cruelty run unchecked, as long as it was hidden from public view.

I couldn't play that game. I was angry, and I was vocal. At home, at school, on the streets, I spoke up every time I saw unfairness. It got me labeled as "the angry child." People told me to shut up, think before I spoke, tame my rage. I tried. I really did. But the more I tried to stifle my anger, the more it burned inside me.

Masked and Muted

Somewhere along the line, I learned to mask it. To mute myself. I watched the people with money, with power, with the gift of smooth words, get away with things that would have destroyed someone like me. I saw kids with the right surnames, the right skin tone, and the right accents breeze through life, while the rest of us learned to keep our heads down. I learned to fear exclusion more than I feared injustice. Because social exclusion, I read once, lights up the same part of your brain as physical pain—a kind of psychic amputation. To be left out is to be cut off from the world. So we learn, early, to do whatever it takes to stay included. For some of us, that means silence.

I won't lie: part of me still admires the wild cards, the ones who say what everyone else is thinking and don't care about the fallout. Sometimes, they get away with it. Sometimes, they get punished. I wonder if they feel the same fear I do—the fear that the door will slam in your face and you'll be left to fend for yourself, alone and exposed to the dangers lurking in the dark.

But most of us, we stuff it down. We hide our anger, our hurt, our opinions. We learn to mute our thoughts and feelings, to keep them locked away where no one can see. We tell ourselves it's for survival. And it is.

The New Generation

Things are changing, though. Kids today—they're better at expressing themselves. They talk about their feelings in ways that make me uncomfortable. They say "I feel angry," and nobody tells them to hush. They cry, they scream, they demand to be heard. Part of me envies them. They haven't learned to be afraid yet, or maybe they're brave enough not to care. I grew up being told to stuff it in, to put on a brave face, to never let anyone see me bleed. Now I watch the next generation erupt—sometimes in rage, sometimes in joy—and I realize I was never taught how to handle that. I don't want to be the person who tells them to put their chin up and move on. I want to listen, to validate, to let them know their anger is not a flaw.

But it's hard. Vulnerability still feels like a risk. Expressing anger still comes with shame, with the fear of being rejected or excluded. I cling to my old habits, even as I try to break them. Sometimes, I succeed. Sometimes, I fail. But I try.

Corporate Rebel

My anger never disappeared. It just got redirected. In the corporate world, I became a rebel. I challenged the rules, the norms, the double standards. Sometimes it cost me—promotions missed, relationships strained, being labeled "difficult." But it also gave me power. There's a kind of authenticity that comes from owning your anger, from refusing to let others define you. I started my own company, built my own team, created a space where I could be myself. I realized that feeling and expressing anger—productively, constructively—is a source of strength, not weakness.

But every time I think about fully opening that door, letting the anger out, I hesitate. What if it's too much? What if people turn away, slam the door, leave me outside to fend for myself? The old fears never really go away. I still wonder why others are allowed to be angry, to have opinions, to speak up—while I'm told to give in, to bend, to be accommodating.

The Double Standard

That's the heart of it, isn't it? The double standard. Men are "passionate." Women are "hysterical." Men are "assertive." Women are "aggressive." When I raise my voice, I'm told to calm down. When I stand my ground, I'm told I'm being difficult. Why should I always be the one to bend? Why do I have to be the bigger person, the peacemaker, the one who smooths things over?

There's a kind of violence in that expectation—a slow, suffocating erasure of self. I see it now, in hindsight. Every time I swallowed my anger, every time I bit my tongue, I chipped away at my own authenticity. I made myself smaller, quieter, more palatable. But the anger never left. It just brewed, waiting for a chance to break through.

The Cost of Silence

Social exclusion is a blade, and we learn to fear it above almost anything else. From a young age, we're taught that belonging is the ultimate prize, and that the price of belonging is silence. They don't say it outright, but you learn it in the pauses, in the sidelong glances, in the way people suddenly stop talking when you enter a room.

I used to think this was just me, or maybe just my family. But it's everywhere. In every society, every workplace, every friendship group, there are unspoken rules about what you're allowed to feel, what you're allowed to say, who gets to be angry and who doesn't. The people with power—money, status, skin tone, charisma—bend the rules to suit themselves. The rest of us learn to adapt, to hide, to blend in.

But living like that comes at a cost. You lose your voice. You lose your spark. You forget what it feels like to be unapologetically yourself.

The Breakthrough

My real breakthrough didn't come from a book or a TED talk or some grand epiphany. It came from reaching the end of my rope. I'd spent years trying to be what everyone else wanted—quiet, agreeable, diplomatic. I'd built a successful company, earned respect, made money. But I was exhausted. The mask was heavy, and the anger was still there, simmering just below the surface.

One day, I decided to stop hiding. I let myself feel the anger, really feel it. I let it wash over me, burn through me, light me up from the inside. And then, for the first time, I tried to express it—not as a weapon, but as a truth. I told my team when I was frustrated. I called out unfairness when I saw it. I stopped apologizing for having feelings.

It was terrifying. I kept waiting for the door to slam, for people to turn away, for the world to punish me for breaking the rules. But something else happened. People started listening. They started telling their own stories, sharing their own frustrations, admitting their own anger. The more honest I was, the more connection I found.

I realized that all those years of silence had created a vacuum—one that was just waiting to be filled with real, messy, authentic emotion. The people around me were hungry for it. They wanted honesty, vulnerability, truth. They wanted permission to feel, to express, to be human.

Owning My Anger

I won't pretend I have it all figured out. There are still days when the old fears come back—when I feel the urge to smooth things over, to bite my tongue, to play nice. But I try to remember that my anger is not a flaw. It's a signal, a call to action, a source of power.

Anger tells me when something is wrong. It pushes me to stand up, to speak out, to demand better. It's not always comfortable, for me or for the people around me. But it's real. And I'd rather be real than safe.

A New Kind of Leadership

I see now that one of the greatest gifts I can give—to myself, to my team, to the next generation—is to model what it looks like to own your anger without letting it own you. To feel deeply, to express honestly, to refuse to apologize for being fully alive.

That doesn't mean lashing out or burning bridges. It means channeling anger into action—using it to fuel change, to set boundaries, to demand respect. It means creating spaces where people can be themselves, where they don't have to hide or pretend or stuff their feelings down.

It means teaching my children, my colleagues, my friends that anger is not the enemy. Silence is.

The Legacy of Authenticity

If there's one thing I hope to leave behind, it's this: you don't have to mute yourself to belong. You don't have to stuff your emotions down to be loved or accepted. You are allowed to be angry. You are allowed to speak up. You are allowed to take up space.

The world will try to tell you otherwise. It will reward the compliant, the agreeable, the silent. But it will never love you for who you are if you keep hiding.

So let yourself be wild. Let yourself be loud. Let yourself feel. And when the anger comes, don't run from it. Listen to it. Honor it. Let it show you where you need to grow, where you need to fight, where you need to break through.

You might be surprised by what happens when you finally let yourself be seen.

Pearls of Insight

- ❖ **Hypocrisy is poison:** Societies, families, and companies that preach one thing and practice another breed anger, alienation, and silence.
- ❖ **Anger is not a flaw:** It's a signal, a source of authenticity, and a catalyst for change—when channeled constructively.
- ❖ **Social exclusion is real pain:** The fear of being left out can silence even the loudest voices, but it's possible to break the cycle.
- ❖ **You don't have to mute yourself:** Authenticity is risky, but the alternative—living half a life—is worse.
- ❖ **The next generation is watching:** Model what it looks like to own your emotions, so they don't have to learn silence as survival.

Reflect & Explore

1. **How were you taught to handle anger?** What messages did you receive about expressing—or suppressing—strong emotions?
2. **Who around you gets to be angry?** Who gets shut down or silenced? Why?
3. **How might you model authentic expression?** In your work, family, or friendships, where could you safely let more of your real feelings show?
4. **What door are you afraid to open?** What would it look like to step through anyway?

Breakthroughs aren't always loud or dramatic. Sometimes, they're a quiet decision to stop hiding and let yourself be seen. But after the mask comes off, what happens next? In the aftermath, I would have to confront the difference between surviving and truly living.

CHAPTER 7
Echoes of Aldgate: Trauma, Humanity, and the Forging of Purpose

What does it feel like when the world you trust explodes in an instant? One ordinary morning in London, I stepped onto a train—and into the heart of a tragedy that would split my life into "before" and "after." In the chaos and the smoke, I learned how quickly a city of strangers can become a lifeline—or a reminder of how alone you can feel in a crowd.

I'd just returned to London, my dreams as fragile as the visa in my passport. I was temping—Personal Assistant to a Managing Director at a tier-one consultancy, a cog in a machine advising a major UK bank on IT transformation. I didn't know it then, but those frantic workshops and strategy sessions were the first flickers of what would become my real passion: facilitation, helping people think together, forging clarity out of chaos.

That morning, July 7th, 2005, started like any other—a rush to be polished and punctual. I left my flat early, nerves dancing in my stomach. My commute was a patchwork: one line, then another. When I reached the platform, I couldn't make out the station clock. For no special reason—just a flicker of impatience—I took three more steps down, closer to the front.

The next train slid in; I stepped on, found a seat, grabbed a free newspaper, and tried to disappear into the page.

The ritual lasted maybe two minutes. The train started, the city receding, and then—boom.

A noise so loud it felt like the world itself had been torn in two. The train shuddered to a halt. At first, it was just stunned silence—a vacuum, a collective holding of breath. Then black, choking smoke began to seep in, thickening the air. Panic erupted. We looked at each other, strangers seconds before, now bound together by something primal. Someone screamed, "Bomb blast."

The air changed. The unspoken London rule—keep your head down, avoid eye contact—evaporated. Scarves were pressed into shaking hands to cover faces. Tissues were offered to strangers, tears wiped from unfamiliar cheeks. Some people froze. Some tried to smash the windows, desperate to escape, only to be stopped by others warning about live electrocuted tracks. The line between us and death was just a set of carriage doors. I realized, slowly and with a kind of sick awe, that the carriage beside mine—the one I would have entered had I not taken those three impulsive steps—was blown. Just blown.

Shock cocooned me. We waited, all pretenses stripped away, for help or for something to make sense. When rescue finally arrived, we were told the lines were safe, and we began to file out—clinging to strangers' hands, walking single-file onto the tracks. That's when the true scale of it hit. The carriage that had exploded was a mangled ruin. Dead bodies lay scattered on the rails. Blood everywhere. I saw a man shaking so hard he couldn't stand, paramedics crouched beside him. My brain rebelled, refusing to take it in, but my body shook and the tears came. I somehow made it out of Aldgate station, each step feeling both impossible and automatic.

Outside, a policeman asked if I was hurt. "Not physically," I whispered, "but mentally…" He nodded grimly—there were buses for the wounded; the rest of us were left to figure it out.

I drifted with a handful of survivors to a Starbucks across the street. My hands shook so much I could barely hold the hot chocolate I ordered. We sat together, this accidental tribe, sipping and watching as, one by one, families and friends arrived to collect their loved ones. Until, finally, I was the only one left. No one to call, no one to come for me. I watched the chaos outside the station, acutely, achingly alone.

Eventually, I mustered the strength to call my employer: I wouldn't make it to the workshop. I called my cousin, my friend Amy, my flatmate. News was coming in on my phone: more bombs, more carnage, buses now targeted. I lived in Harrow, Zone 6—miles from Aldgate. The tube was shut down. Walking was the only option, a journey that could take the rest of the day.

I started out, disoriented, wandering in circles, sometimes joining others from the train—silent companions for a few blocks—before we peeled off, each to our own destination. Somehow, I ended up near the consultancy office, exhausted and hollowed out. The manager I'd been assisting spotted me and rushed over, hugging me, letting me call my parents in Kenya. I lied, told them I was fine, at work, safe. I pictured them, glued to CNN, oceans away, powerless. I couldn't bear to add to their pain.

Then came the moment that still stings: a senior woman from the consultancy approached, her voice clipped and cold. "Can you go sit in a corner?" she said. "Your presence is disturbing people from working." Stunned, I moved, feeling smaller than I thought possible. There, in the corner, a Black woman from the bank saw me. She fetched me a hot chocolate, stayed close, watched over me. The contrast was searing: inhuman detachment on one hand, simple human kindness on the other. I looked out the window and saw crowds already starting the long walk home. I decided to do the same, but needed to rest first.

As I gathered myself, a call came through—one of the last before mobile lines were blocked. David, an old colleague from Zurich, found me. Years before, on 9/11, I had comforted him. Now he returned the favor, picking me up in a taxi, collecting others along the way. He offered to take me to his parents' home for safety, but I insisted on returning to my flat, craving the familiar comfort of my childhood friend.

When I arrived home, she barely looked up from the news. "I hope you're not going to break down and cry," she said. "I've seen enough of that on TV all day." Just like that, the possibility of comfort was gone. I retreated to my room, more alone than ever. The next morning, desperate for peace, I made my way to the Swaminarayan temple in Neasden. I sat in the stillness, letting it hold what I couldn't.

Something shifted inside me. The trauma was real, but so was a new kind of resolve. I wasn't going to let this break me. I'd fought too hard to build my life here. I couldn't go home. If I left now, I knew I'd never come back, and my dreams would die on the tarmac at Heathrow.

But guilt gnawed at me—a flawed logic, but powerful. I remembered the protests against the Iraq war, how I hadn't joined them, how I'd let myself believe I couldn't make a difference. Now, in the aftermath, I wondered: If I had marched, if I'd raised my voice, would any of this have changed? The question haunted me, irrational but relentless.

Worse, my flatmate spread news of my ordeal back in Nakuru. My parents heard through the grapevine. My father called, heartbroken, desperate to bring me home. I made him stay. It was an act of will, a stubborn belief that survival meant pressing on, not retreating.

I went back to work, my desk moved out of sight. The manager docked my pay for the day of the bombing. The company, no doubt, billed the client full price for the workshop I'd missed. The only kindness came from the woman at the bank, who steered me toward counseling. Therapy became a lifeline. With help, I found the courage to move out, to finally live alone, to claim a small patch of safety in a world that didn't always offer it.

For years, PTSD shadowed me. Certain sounds, certain crowds, brought it all back. My mind, protective and sly, blocked out the details. For two years, I worked near Aldgate, using the station daily, never realizing where I was until one day, eating lunch by the window, I looked up and everything rushed back. The mind protects itself until it can't.

Through all this, I saw the best and worst of humanity. Strangers in crisis became rescuers, comforters, friends. Others, colleagues and even friends, recoiled, pushed me to the margins, made my pain an inconvenience. It shaped me. It made me notice who is left out, who is struggling. It forged a fierce sense of purpose: to show up, scars and all, for others who might one day find themselves at the edge.

Eventually, I became a management consultant myself. I chose to work only with boutique Management Consultancy that put people at the center. Now, running my own human-centered design consultancy, I try to make impact by design, with people always at the heart. I can't undo the past, but I can honor it by serving, by building bridges, by insisting on empathy as the cornerstone of leadership.

Trauma doesn't just leave scars—it strips away illusions, clarifies what matters, and forges a new sense of purpose. I couldn't undo what happened, but I could choose to show up—wounded, yes, but wiser and more determined to build a world where empathy is not an afterthought, but the foundation of leadership

Pearls of Insight

- ❖ **Trauma clarifies what matters most.**
- ❖ **Purpose is found in choosing to show up, scars and all.**
- ❖ **Trauma's Long Shadow:** Profoundly traumatic events can have lasting psychological impacts, including PTSD, memory suppression, and resurfacing during times of stress.

- ❖ **Humanity in Crisis:** Moments of extreme crisis reveal the full spectrum of human behaviour—from extraordinary compassion and solidarity among strangers to shocking indifference or self-preservation.
- ❖ **The Body Remembers:** The mind may block traumatic memories as a coping mechanism, but the body and subconscious often retain the imprint, which can resurface unexpectedly.
- ❖ **Invalidation Compounds Trauma:** Having one's experience dismissed or minimized by others, especially by those expected to offer support, can significantly hinder the healing process.
- ❖ **Purpose Forged in Fire:** Deeply challenging or traumatic experiences can sometimes become the catalyst for discovering a profound sense of purpose, often focused on preventing similar suffering or fostering positive change.
- ❖ **Seeking Support is Strength:** Recognizing the need for and accepting professional help (like counselling) is a crucial step in processing trauma and rebuilding resilience.
- ❖ **Authenticity in Healing:** True healing often involves integrating the traumatic experience into one's life narrative, not by erasing it, but by finding meaning and strength from it.

Reflect & Explore

1. **Moments of Crisis:** Think about a challenging or crisis moment in your own life (it doesn't have to be on the scale of a bombing). What surprised you about your own reactions or the reactions of others? What did you learn about human nature?
2. **The Impact of Invalidation:** Have you ever had an experience where your feelings or perceptions were

dismissed by others? How did that make you feel, and how did it affect your ability to process the situation?
3. **Finding Purpose in Pain:** Can you identify a difficult experience in your past that, in retrospect, has shaped your values, your purpose, or your compassion for others in a meaningful way?

Surviving Aldgate changed the way I saw myself and the world. But healing is never linear. As I moved forward, I would discover that the journey from trauma to purpose is paved with both setbacks and small, hard-won victories—each one a step toward reclaiming my story.

CHAPTER 8
The Sisterhood Paradox

What if the greatest challenge for women in high-stakes industries isn't the men, but the myth of automatic sisterhood? In the high-rise towers of finance, I learned that scarcity doesn't always unite—it can turn allies into rivals, and silence into survival.

When people imagine being a woman in tech or finance, they tend to picture a kind of built-in camaraderie. "You must all stick together," they say, as if sisterhood is the natural state when you're outnumbered. In reality, being the only woman—or one of the lonely few—in a high-stakes, high-pressure industry exposes you to the messy, complicated, and sometimes brutal truth about female allyship and rivalry. Scarcity breeds competition, but real power comes from lifting each other up. That sounds simple. It isn't.

The Myth of Automatic Allyship

Let's start with the myth. From the outside, it looks like we're all on the same side—the "sisters in arms" cliché, women's networks, diversity panels, glossy marketing campaigns full of smiling female VPs. In my early career, I bought into it. I wanted to believe that every woman I met in the City would have my back. That we'd trade war stories, share advice, warn each other about the landmines, help each other climb. And sometimes, yes, that happened. But just as often, it didn't.

I remember my first week at the tier-one global investment bank in London, I had made a massive career jump. This was the pinnacle, or so I thought—the place where ambitious women were not just welcomed but celebrated. The branding was masterful. They paraded impressive female leaders from London and New York, women who looked like they'd never had a hair out of place or a moment of doubt. I felt like I'd won the lottery.

The reality was grittier. My department dealt in complex, high-value OTC derivatives—minimum trade, $100 million. Next door, the standardized products team worked on much smaller deals. On my very first day, a senior Director leaned in and said, "We don't really talk to the standardized function. We're better than them." It was a casual aside, meant as a joke, but it landed hard. There it was: the subtle hierarchy, the sense that belonging was fragile and conditional, even within the same company.

That was my first lesson: scarcity changes the game. There were only a handful of women at my level, and every promotion, every coveted project, felt like a zero-sum contest. If one of us got ahead, it often felt like there was one less chair for the rest. Sometimes, we banded together. More often, we kept our heads down, careful not to make too much noise, wary of stepping on each other's toes.

The Honeymoon Phase—and Its End

The bank had done its homework. They knew how to make you feel special, part of an elite club. Early on, I was invited to panels, coffee catchups, and roundtables with female leaders. I met women at the top, women who told stories about breaking the glass ceiling, about outsmarting the boys' club, about mentoring the next generation. It was intoxicating, and I wanted so badly to believe it was the whole truth.

But the shine wore off fast. The hours were relentless. Arriving at 7 am drew sarcastic comments about "sleeping in."

Leaving at 7 pm got you branded as "lazy." You were expected to have read the Financial Times before you walked in and to log back on after dinner for late-night calls with New York. Weekends and holidays? Don't even think about unplugging.

Workload aside, there was a constant, low-level pressure to prove yourself—not just as a banker, but as a woman. I couldn't shake the feeling that I was representing my entire gender, every time I opened my mouth. If I made a mistake, it wasn't just my reputation on the line. It was the next woman's, too.

When Scarcity Breeds Competition

Here's the thing about scarcity: it doesn't just make you defensive. It can make you ruthless. I saw it everywhere, but never more clearly than in my interactions with other women. Most of us wanted to support each other. But in an environment where only a handful of women got ahead, rivalry was inevitable.

One woman in particular stands out—a ginger-haired sales director, sharp as a tack and twice as quick. She could be charming when she needed something, but if you stood in her way, she became your worst nightmare. One night, after a long evening out, she reviewed one of my request for proposal (RFP) documents and tore it to shreds—redlining whole sections, calling my work incompetent, and firing off an email to every senior director in the department. The implication was clear: she was the hero, staying late to fix my mess. The next day, I sat down with her, point by point, and calmly explained that her "corrections" were wrong—she'd misread the document in her drunken haze. I asked her to send a clarifying email to the group. She refused. "That would make me look bad," she said, as if that settled it.

It didn't matter that I was right. The damage was done. The image of my work bleeding red ink stuck in everyone's mind. Truth didn't stand a chance against perception.

I wish I could say this was an isolated incident, some outlier in an otherwise supportive environment. It wasn't. As the pressure ramped up—more RFPs, more clients, more late nights—the microaggressions multiplied. Mistakes were spotlighted, scrutinized, amplified. When management's favorites slipped up, their errors were quietly swept under the rug. When I stumbled, it was in full view, dissected by a room of people who seemed invested in my failure.

Eventually, I confronted the sales director about her behavior. She didn't flinch. "I'm doing you a favor," she said. "When I started here, I was bullied until I learned to be tough. Sink or swim." That was her version of mentorship—throwing me in the deep end and calling it a kindness.

The Cost of Silence

The real heartbreak, though, wasn't the overt rivalry. It was the silence. I'll never forget the day we said goodbye to a pregnant colleague—one of the most hard-working, dedicated women I'd ever met. As she walked out, belly round and glowing, a Managing Director turned to another and said, "Well, we wrote her off the day she got married. Knew she'd have kids and move on." Several others nodded. No one—least of all the other women—said a word. We all just stared at our screens, pretending not to hear.

That silence was suffocating. It was the sound of survival, of women who had learned the hard way that speaking up rarely paid off. And it was a silence I found myself complicit in, more often than I'd like to admit.

The cumulative effect was devastating. I was crying almost every night, my stress levels through the roof, my confidence in shreds. My PTSD, dormant for years, came roaring back. I felt like I was falling apart, but I couldn't let anyone see me bleed. After all, I was supposed to be one of the "lucky ones"—a Vice President, well-paid, with a CV that sparkled.

Breaking Point—and Breaking Free

In the end, it wasn't the work that broke me. It was the culture. After weeks of barely holding it together, I quit. The bank walked me out, as is custom, and left me with a paid notice period to process the shock.

A week later, I found out I was pregnant. The joy was immediate, but so was the panic. Unemployed, facing the prospect of job-hunting while visibly pregnant, I wondered if I'd made a catastrophic mistake.

But then I remembered that pregnant colleague, dismissed the moment she was deemed likely to "move on." I realized that no matter how hard I worked, I would have been written off too. Staying would have meant enduring pregnancy in a place that saw me as disposable. Quitting, I realized, was an act of self-preservation.

The job search was brutal. My confidence was shot, and rejection after rejection stung. But then, a friend I'd helped years before mentioned a contracting role. It felt risky, but what did I have to lose? I interviewed, leaned on connections from happier days, and landed the job.

The contrast was staggering. Suddenly, I was working with people who cared. The work was hard, sometimes even harder than before, but it was collaborative, supportive, fun. I worked 8 to 5. Evenings and weekends were mine again. No one stole credit for my work. My contributions were recognized, respected. I felt human.

And the ultimate irony? As a contractor, I paid myself enough to take a proper maternity leave—something that would have been impossible in my old role.

Within two years, I'd gone from the most toxic environment of my life to the most fulfilling. Nothing about my skill set had changed. The difference was the people, the culture, the choice to support rather than compete.

The Real Meaning of Sisterhood

Looking back, what strikes me most is how easily scarcity can turn us against each other. When there are so few seats at the table, every woman becomes a rival by default. The system is rigged to make us compete, to measure our worth against each other instead of against the real problem: a culture that only allows a handful of us to succeed.

But it doesn't have to be that way. I've seen what real sisterhood looks like—the quiet acts of kindness, the whispered warnings, the shared laughs after a brutal meeting. These moments are rare, but they're powerful. They're the reason some women survive, and even thrive, in environments designed to break them.

Allyship is a choice, not a guarantee. I wish I could tell you that every woman will root for you, that every "women's network" is the real deal. But the truth is, allyship takes work. It means risking your own position sometimes. It means speaking up when it's easier to stay silent. It means remembering that your success is not diminished by someone else's win.

It also means paying it forward. When I finally found my footing again, I made a promise to myself: I'd do everything I could to be the woman who helps, not the one who hoards. Sometimes that means mentoring someone, sometimes it's just a word of encouragement, sometimes it's sharing the truth about what's really going on behind the glossy branding.

Pearls of Insight

- ❖ **Scarcity breeds competition:** abundance creates true sisterhood. Whenever possible, choose abundance—there is room for more than one of us at the top.
- ❖ **Allyship is a choice, not a guarantee:** It takes real effort and sometimes courage to support other women, especially when the system tries to pit us against each other.

Reflect & Explore

1. **When have you experienced competition or support among women?** How did it shape your view of what real allyship looks like?
2. **Who can you encourage, mentor, or support this week?** What small action could make a difference for another woman coming up behind you?

Leaving behind the illusions and heartbreak of false sisterhood, I stepped into a new chapter—one where I would have to redefine success, rebuild my confidence, and discover what it truly meant to lead with integrity, both for myself and for those coming after me.

PART II
NAVIGATING SYSTEMS, BIAS, AND BURNOUT

CHAPTER 9
If You Knew You Were Intelligent...

If you knew—truly knew—you were intelligent, what would you dare to do? For women of color from immigrant families, this question isn't just provocative—it's revolutionary. It challenges the quiet scripts of doubt and the weight of history, demanding you trust the mind you've built instead of shrinking to fit someone else's expectations.

The Question That Changes Everything

If you knew you were intelligent, what thoughts would you dare to have?

It's a question that doesn't just hang in the air—it lands with a thud, heavy with all the history, all the doubt, all the possibility that's been bottled up inside you for years. It's a question that strips away the polite modesty and the armor of hard work and gets right to the core: Do you trust the mind you've built, or are you just playing a role handed down by someone else's expectations?

For women of colour—especially those from immigrant, working-class families—this question hits different. Intelligence is supposed to be the great equalizer, the thing nobody can take from you. But what if the world, over and over, tells you that your intelligence is only as good as your willingness to act small?

What if every time you dare to believe in yourself, there's a chorus of voices, inside and outside, asking: Who do you think you are?

The Desert and the Dream

My story starts in the Rann of Kutch, a place as harsh as it is beautiful. My family were poor farmers, our lives measured out in seasons of drought and hope, the horizon always shimmering with the promise of something better. It's a place where dreams are practical things—like seeds, you plant them in the dust and hope the rains will come.

For my father, the dream was education. Not just for himself, but for his daughters. It was a radical idea. In our community, girls weren't supposed to dream too big. But necessity has a way of upending tradition. My family, like so many others, crossed oceans to Africa, chasing the possibility of a new life. We carried little but our stories and the conviction that hard work and learning could change everything.

Education wasn't a luxury. It was survival. It was the only way to rewrite the script handed to us by circumstance and history. My father broke rules, faced down scorn from relatives and neighbors, and insisted that his daughters would have every chance the world could offer. He was stubborn about it. Fierce. He didn't just talk—he acted, no matter the cost.

That's where my foundation was built. Not in privilege, but in the wild, hungry hope that comes from having nothing to lose.

Working Twice as Hard (For Half the Credit)

If you grow up like this, you learn early that work is your ticket out. Not just any work—relentless, disciplined, often invisible labour. You learn to keep your head down, to collect gold stars, to be grateful for every opportunity even when you know you earned it ten times over.

But there's a catch. No matter how hard you work, there's always a whisper of doubt. The world doesn't hand out credibility cards to girls like you. You get used to being underestimated—sometimes kindly, sometimes not. "She's diligent, reliable, a hard worker." Rarely do you hear: "She's brilliant."

So you keep working. You collect degrees, certifications, glowing performance reviews. You become indispensable, but not quite "exceptional"—at least not in the eyes of those who write the rules. You wonder: Is this the ceiling? Am I just here to serve, to execute, to be the safe pair of hands behind someone else's vision?

The Invisible Tax

The cost of being a woman of colour in professional spaces isn't just measured in missed promotions or smaller paychecks—though those are real enough. The bigger tax is psychological. It's the way you start to internalize the world's low expectations, the way you police your own ambitions before anyone else can cut them down.

You hear it in the microaggressions: "You speak such good English!" "You're so articulate!" "You don't seem Indian." You see it in the meetings where your ideas are ignored, then repackaged by someone else and suddenly "innovative." You feel it in the isolation, the sense that you're always auditioning, never quite belonging.

If you're not careful, you start to believe the feedback loop. You stop taking risks. You shrink your hopes to fit the box you've been handed. You call it "being realistic," but really, it's just self-preservation.

The Myth of Deserving

There comes a moment—a handful of moments, really—when you're forced to ask: Why do I want to be recognized? Why do I feel I deserve an award, a promotion, a seat at the table?

For a long time, I thought wanting recognition was selfish, even shameful. Good girls don't ask for attention; they let their work speak for itself. But the truth is, the world doesn't always listen. Sometimes you have to speak up, to claim your space, not just for yourself, but for everyone who comes after you.

So I started to interrogate my own motives. Was it ego? Maybe a little. After years of delivering value, making an impact, helping to build highly impactful digital products that lasted, I wanted someone to notice. I wanted to be seen. But it's more than that.

Recognition brings social credibility. It opens doors, attracts clients, creates opportunities to do meaningful work. It helps you build a sustainable business, to be known as a thought leader, to shape the direction of your industry. It's about having a voice—not for its own sake, but to deepen the human-technology connection, to create experiences that lift everyone up.

And underneath it all, there's the question of representation. When you grow up never seeing anyone who looks like you at the front of the room, you start to wonder if you belong there at all. If I want to change that for the next generation, I have to step up, to be visible, to show what's possible.

The Absence of Role Models

I loved science as a child—physics, chemistry, computers, the way the world fit together. But the message was clear: "Leave the computers to the boys." There were no Indian women in the textbooks, no brown girls at the science fairs. The few women I saw in leadership roles seemed hardened by the journey, forced to play by rules that punished any hint of softness or solidarity.

You can't be what you can't see. So I tried to become the thing I needed—a leader who didn't just survive the system, but changed it. Someone who made space for others, who mentored, who lifted as she climbed. Someone who could be looked up to, not just for what she achieved, but for how she achieved it.

Risk and Resilience

My career has never been a straight line. I was the nerdy kid who built telescopes out of cardboard, who spent weekends taking apart a watch and putting them back together. School in Africa taught conformity—one right answer, no room for questions. But curiosity is stubborn. I read everything I could get my hands on, studied how things worked, and started to see the patterns beneath the surface.

As I moved into the professional world, I learned to apply that same lens to organizations. Why do we do things this way? Who benefits? What's broken, and how can we fix it? I became a problem-solver, a systems thinker. I learned that leadership isn't about having all the answers—it's about asking better questions, about making space for experimentation and growth.

But none of this would have happened if I hadn't learned to take risks. Real confidence is built on the ruins of risk. Every time I spoke up in a meeting, every time I challenged a process or put myself forward for a role I wasn't "supposed" to want, I was building a new foundation—not just for myself, but for everyone watching.

Battling Bias, Building Belief

It would be a lie to say I never doubted my intelligence. There were plenty of times when the world's skepticism seeped in—when a manager questioned my judgment, when a peer "mansplained" my own work back to me, when a client assumed I was the junior on the team. There were times I almost believed them.

But every time, I came back to something my father taught me: Intelligence isn't just what you know, it's how you grow. It's not about having all the answers, but about being willing to learn, to adapt, to keep moving forward even when the ground is shaky.

So I started acting on my intelligence. I stopped waiting for permission. I took on projects that scared me, stepped into leadership roles before I felt ready, said yes to opportunities that seemed out of reach. And every time I succeeded, every time I failed and got up again, I was proving—to myself, if not to the world—that I belonged.

The Real Reason for Recognition

So why do I want the award? Why do I want my name on the list, my face on the stage?

Because recognition is about visibility, and visibility is about possibility. When you're seen, you're not just making space for yourself—you're holding the door open for everyone who's ever felt invisible. You're sending a message, loud and clear: You belong here, too.

It's about credibility, yes. But it's also about impact. About building a business that matters, about connecting technology and humanity in ways that lift everyone up. About making sure no one is left behind.

And it's about representation. I want the girls who love science, the women who doubt themselves, the leaders who feel alone, to see what's possible. I want them to know that you don't have to become ruthless to succeed, that you can lead with empathy and courage and still make it to the top.

Paying It Forward

This isn't just a career. It's a commitment. I mentor women and marginalized individuals, guide children from low socioeconomic backgrounds, drive initiatives for indigenous engagement and decarbonization. I serve on boards, chair awards programs, create platforms for youth. I do it because I know what it's like to walk into a room and feel like you don't belong. I do it because I want to be the change I needed.

I'm not interested in collecting followers. I want to create more leaders. I want to show that you can climb high and stay grounded, that ambition and humility aren't opposites but partners.

If you follow the thread far enough, every ambition leads to a deeper purpose.

And at the deepest level: Because I want to be the role model I never had, for the next generation of women, for every kid who's ever felt out of place. I want to prove that your origins don't have to limit your future, that you can rise without leaving your values behind.

Intelligence Is Action

There's a myth that intelligence is something you're born with—a static thing, measured in test scores and degrees. But real intelligence is what you do with what you know. It's how you adapt, how you learn, how you risk.

You prove your intelligence every time you act on it. Every time you step out of your comfort zone, every time you trust your instincts, every time you refuse to shrink for someone else's comfort.

The Risks Worth Taking

If you knew—truly knew—you were intelligent, what would you do differently? Would you speak up more? Would you take that job, start that business, write that book? Would you dare to dream a little bigger, to ask for more, to expect to be at the center of the story instead of on the margins?

For me, the answer has been to risk visibility. To put my name forward, even when I'm scared. To claim the credit I've earned, to own my story. It hasn't always been easy. There have been setbacks, failures, moments when I wanted to disappear.

But every time I chose courage over comfort, I grew—not just in skill, but in self-belief.

The Power of Representation

When I look back at my journey, the thing I'm most proud of isn't the awards or the titles. It's the emails from women who say, "Because of you, I believed I could do it too." It's the students who see themselves in my story and decide to keep going. It's the colleagues who find the courage to speak up because they saw me do it first.

Representation isn't just a buzzword. It's a lifeline. When you see someone who looks like you, who shares your background, your struggles, your hopes—you believe a little more in your own possibilities.

Grounded Ambition

Ambition isn't a dirty word. Neither is service. The best leaders I know are the ones who remember where they came from, who stay connected to the people they serve, who measure their success by the impact they have on others.

I try to stay grounded in my roots—in the desert that taught me resilience, in the sacrifices of my family, in the communities that shaped me. I try to use my ambition not just to climb, but to lift. Not just to win, but to transform.

You are more intelligent than you know. The world may not always recognize it, but you can. When you choose to act on your intelligence—to risk, to grow, to claim your place—you don't just change your own life; you rewrite the script for everyone who follows.

Pearls of Insight

- ❖ **Motivation is Layered:** The drive for recognition is complex, shaped by ego, ambition, and a deep desire to make a difference and be seen.
- ❖ **Overcoming Adversity Fuels Purpose:** The hardest battles can become the strongest fuel for purposeful leadership and service.
- ❖ **Representation Requires Visibility:** True impact comes from being seen, from standing up and modeling what's possible for those who follow.
- ❖ **Be the Change:** Real leadership is about embodying the values you wish to see, becoming the role model you once needed.
- ❖ **Grounded Ambition:** Ambition is most powerful—and most sustainable—when it's rooted in humility and a commitment to lifting others up.

Reflect & Explore

1. **Daring Thoughts:** If you fully embraced your intelligence and capabilities today, what "daring thoughts" about your potential, your ambitions, or the impact you could make would you allow yourself to have?
2. **Your "Why" Chain:** Choose one significant goal or ambition you hold. Ask yourself "Why?" repeatedly, digging deeper with each answer, until you uncover the core motivations driving you.
3. **Role Model Reflection:** Who were your role models growing up (or who are they now)? What specific qualities or actions inspired you? How might you embody those qualities for someone else?

If daring to believe in my intelligence was the first step, the next would be learning how to use that belief to break barriers—not just for myself, but for those whose voices are still waiting to be heard.

CHAPTER 10
Accents and Superiority

Step into any global boardroom and you'll hear it before you see it: the subtle hierarchy of accents, where the way you speak can open doors—or quietly shut them. For years, I learned that my voice was more than communication; it was a passport or a barrier, a mark of pride or a trigger for shame. Whose voice gets to belong, and whose is always "other"?

The Invisible Hierarchy of Sound

Walk into any global conference room, and you'll hear it before you see it: the hierarchy that language and accent quietly enforce. It's in the way voices are heard, the way ideas are weighed, the way power shifts—sometimes subtly, sometimes jarringly—with nothing more than a turn of phrase or a certain lilt. Most people will tell you that language is just about communication, but anyone who's ever felt their accent become a barrier knows it's so much more. It's a marker of identity and, too often, a currency of belonging.

As a woman of color who's navigated boardrooms and brainstorms from Europe to Australia, I've learned this the hard way. The way you speak can open doors or slam them shut. It can be a source of pride or a trigger for shame. And learning to value your own voice, with all its history and imperfections, is not just self-acceptance—it's a quiet act of rebellion.

The Scene: West Tech Fest, Perth

Let me take you to West Tech Fest in Perth—a swirling convergence of ideas, startups, and ambition. It was the kind of event that promised to flatten hierarchies, to put everyone on equal footing in the name of "innovation." A delegation had arrived from India, a country that, despite all its complexity and contradictions, is undeniably a powerhouse in technology and ideas.

But what unfolded was something else: a sad, familiar dance of optics over substance. I watched as members of the Indian group darted from one white attendee to another, snapping photos, collecting business cards, barely pausing to learn or engage. It was so frantic, it bordered on farce. I tried to connect, wanting to talk strategy, to see if there was a chance for real collaboration. Instead, the leader—a woman with no time for small talk—waved me off and lavished her attention on a 14-year-old boy from a local startup showcase. In that moment, my brown skin made me invisible.

Later, a friend—another Indian woman, seasoned and sharp—offered her explanation. "She needs proof for her bosses back home," she said. "Photos with white people, business cards—those are what count. Not us." That stung. But it made sense. In India, she explained, the currency of global engagement is still white validation. Photos with white faces mean you were moving in the right circles, making the right connections. Photos with fellow Indians? In a country of over a billion brown people, it means nothing.

This wasn't just about ambition or networking. It was about a deeply internalized belief in what—and who—matters. It was about the legacy of colonialism, alive and well in the way we chase approval, in the way we measure our worth.

The Weight of an Accent

It's impossible to separate this scene from the broader context of how accents operate in global spaces. For as long as I can remember, I've noticed how quickly people from India, Kenya, Zimbabwe, and other former colonies adapt their speech when they land in the UK, Australia, or the US. Sometimes it's conscious, sometimes it's not. Within weeks, their "Rs" soften, their vowels shift, their sentences fill with borrowed idioms.

But look at it the other way. A British person born and raised in Mumbai will almost always keep their British accent, no matter how long they stay. Their way of speaking is never questioned, never mocked, never seen as something to be corrected. It's the default. The gold standard.

Why is that? Why do some of us bend over backwards to fit in, while others don't have to give it a second thought? Why do we feel pressure to "neutralize" our accents, to sound more "global," while others are free to remain themselves, wherever they go?

The answer, I think, is buried in centuries of history. Colonialism didn't just redraw borders; it rewired brains. It left entire populations with a subtle, insidious sense of inferiority. We learned—sometimes without being taught—that the closer we sounded to the colonizer, the more legitimate we became. Our own accents, our languages, became markers of backwardness. Something to be shed, not celebrated.

The Superiority Complex—Up Close

This isn't just theory. I've lived it. Years ago, while house-hunting in Reading, UK, I met a white man who'd been on jobseeker's allowance for forty years. He could barely read or write. And yet, he looked at me—a brown woman, a university graduate, a professional—and questioned whether I was "qualified" to buy a home. He made it clear that his place in the world was secure, that he could "chill out" and collect benefits, because of who he was and where he came from.

That's what entitlement looks like up close. It's not always loud or aggressive. Sometimes it's just a shrug, a smirk, a sense of effortless superiority. It's knowing you can belong without trying, that the system is built to recognize you, to serve you, to protect your place.

Contrast that with the Indian delegation in Perth, desperately collecting proof of proximity to whiteness. It's the same dynamic, flipped. On one side, there's an unshakable belief in your right to take up space. On the other, a restless anxiety about whether you deserve to be there at all.

Internalized Colonialism: The Inheritance No One Wants

Even though I was born long after India's independence, the shadow of colonialism was everywhere. It was in the way teachers corrected my pronunciation, the way relatives praised "good English," the way Bollywood villains always had thick, "local" accents while the heroes spoke with urbane, Westernized polish. It was in the jokes, the commercials, the stories we told ourselves about who was smart, who was worthy, who was beautiful.

No one said it outright, but the message was clear: white was better, British was best, and your own voice was something to be hidden or "improved." I internalized it. Most of us did. We tried to speak softer, slower, less noticeably. We learned to apologize for our parents' accents, to wince when call center workers were mocked on TV.

What makes it worse is that this hierarchy isn't just between nations. It plays out within our own communities—through colorism, through caste, through the endless ranking of whose English is "proper" and whose is "vernacular." Even as we climb the ladder, we drag these old ideas with us.

Stereotypes and the Persistence of the Old Narrative

Despite everything India has achieved in tech, science, medicine, and business, the old stereotypes die hard. We are still, in many Western imaginations, a country of call centers, snake charmers, and cheap labour. We are order-takers, not leaders. Our accent is a punchline, not a point of pride.

This gap between perception and reality isn't just frustrating. It's damaging. It keeps doors closed. It limits opportunity. And it seeps into how we see ourselves, even when we know better.

The Power of Representation

Sometimes, though, the world shifts. You see it in headlines: Indian CEOs at Google, Microsoft, Twitter. A British Prime Minister of Indian origin. Women like Leena Nair leading Chanel. These stories matter—not just because they break the glass ceiling, but because they rewrite what's possible.

When you read about Satya Nadella or Sundar Pichai, you see a different kind of leadership—one that's collaborative, empathetic, global. You see companies transformed, cultures changed. You see what happens when someone brings their whole self—their accent, their heritage, their worldview—to the table.

These role models aren't just symbols. They're proof that the old hierarchies can be challenged, that the weight of history isn't immovable.

The Global Stage and the Optics of Success

Events like the Ambani wedding—lavish, unapologetic, global—are more than just celebrations. They're statements. They're about showing the world a different narrative: India as a source of wealth, culture, and power, not just labour. And predictably, the Western response is often patronizing, focused on poverty or "wasting" resources. The double standard is glaring. When a Western billionaire spends on a yacht or a moonshot, it's ambition. When an Indian family does it, it's extravagance.

But these spectacles, for all their complexity, are also about reclaiming pride. They're about saying, "We belong on this stage. Our way is valid. Our stories matter."

The Journey from Shame to Pride

I wasn't always proud of my accent. There were years when I tried to hide it, to round off the edges, to fit the mold. I winced when people repeated my words back to me in mockery, or when my parents' English was met with smirks. I felt the sting of being seen as a worker, never a leader.

But slowly, things began to shift. Part of it was seeing people like me in places of power. Part of it was learning the value of my own perspective—the way my background made me resilient, adaptable, creative. And part of it was pure stubbornness. Why should I apologize for the story in my voice? Why should I shrink to fit someone else's idea of "normal"?

Embracing the Accent: An Act of Resistance

There's something radical about deciding to own your accent. To let your voice ring out, unedited, in rooms where you were once told to keep quiet. It's a way of saying: I am enough. My story, my heritage, my way of speaking—they're all assets, not liabilities.

The way I speak is a map of everywhere I've been—India, Africa, UK, Europe and Australia. My words carry the weight of my family, my mentors, my community. To erase that would be to erase myself.

The Challenge of Reclaiming the Narrative

But let's be real: it's not easy. There are still moments of doubt, still rooms where the old hierarchies whisper that you don't belong. There are still jokes, still assumptions, still the subtle pressure to "neutralize" yourself.

The work is ongoing. It's about choosing, every day, to value your own voice. It's about mentoring others, about calling out bias when you see it, about building spaces where difference isn't just tolerated but celebrated.

It means having the courage to challenge stereotypes—to point out when someone's idea of "professionalism" is just code for assimilation. It means being the first to speak up, even when your voice shakes.

Your accent isn't just a sound—it's a living testament to your journey, your survival, and your heritage. Every time you refuse to shrink your voice, you chip away at old hierarchies and make space for others to do the same. The world needs your story, in your own words, spoken with the full weight of where you've been.

Pearls of Insight

- ❖ **Perception vs. Reality in Global Engagement:** So much of what passes for "success" in international spaces is about optics, not substance. True impact comes from real connection, not just photo ops.
- ❖ **Accents as Markers of Identity and Power:** The way we speak can signal belonging or difference, power or marginalization. The choice to embrace your accent is a choice to embrace your story.
- ❖ **Internalized Colonialism:** Colonial histories shape how we see ourselves and others, creating invisible hierarchies that persist long after independence.
- ❖ **Stereotypes Obscure Progress:** Outdated ideas can linger, even when reality has moved on. It's up to us to challenge these narratives, to tell new stories.

❖ **Representation Shifts Narratives:** Every time someone from a marginalized background claims a place at the top, it changes the story for everyone else.

Your Turn: Reflect & Explore

1. **Accent Awareness:** Have you ever changed your way of speaking to fit in, to be understood, or to avoid embarrassment? What did it feel like? What did you gain—and what did you lose—in the process? Think, too, about the reverse: have you met people who refuse to change, who hold onto their accent as a badge of honor? What does that say about power and belonging?
2. **Challenging Stereotypes:** What's the stereotype about your community or culture that bothers you most? How does it line up with your reality—or not? When have you seen someone defy that stereotype, and what impact did it have?
3. **Shifting Perceptions:** Can you recall a moment—a headline, a movie, a leader's appointment—that made you feel proud of your heritage? What was it about that moment that felt like a turning point? What role do visibility and representation play in shifting how the world sees us—and how we see ourselves?

Owning my voice was only the beginning. Next, I would have to learn how to use it—to challenge assumptions, claim space, and lead with the confidence that my story, and my way of telling it, truly mattered.

CHAPTER 11
The Unspoken Barrier—Why Women of Colour Don't Feel Safe

Ask a roomful of professionals why innovation stalls, and you'll hear the usual suspects—funding, strategy, talent. But the real culprit is quieter, more corrosive, and almost never named out loud: the absence of psychological safety. For women of colour, this invisible force is compounded by the intersecting burdens of racism and sexism, shaping every meeting, every risk, and every idea you're too afraid to share.

The Silent Cost of Safety for Women of Colour

Psychological safety is sometimes reduced to a buzzword, but in reality, it's as vital as shelter—especially for women of colour, who often face unique challenges. It's knowing you can show up as your full self—voice your ideas, name your fears, challenge the obvious—without being punished, mocked, or sidelined. For women of colour, this means not having to worry that speaking up will be misinterpreted as being "aggressive" or "difficult," or that their concerns will be dismissed or ignored.

Why Safety Matters More Than You Think

Abraham Maslow got it right: before you can dream big, you need to feel safe. For women of colour, safety is not just about avoiding physical harm or job loss, but about not being subjected to microaggressions, racism, or tokenism. Most organizations reward conformity, not candor, and this is felt even more acutely by women of colour, who are often underrepresented in leadership and decision-making roles.

The Many Faces of Fear—Through an Intersectional Lens

Safety is not just physical. For women of colour, psychological safety is threatened by:

Fear of being labeled as a troublemaker or "diversity hire" for voicing dissent or naming injustice.

Reluctance to report racism, discrimination, or harassment due to distrust in reporting systems and fear of retaliation—women of colour in some studies found it very difficult to report such incidents.

The burden of "onlyness" and tokenism, where women of colour are expected to represent all people of their background, increasing the pressure and scrutiny they face.

Microaggressions and subtle forms of exclusion that accumulate over time, undermining confidence and well-being.

My Story: The Unspoken Barrier for Women of Colour

As a facilitator, I've seen how the absence of psychological safety silences not just ideas, but entire identities. For women of colour, the stakes are higher. They may hesitate to speak up, fearing their contributions will be dismissed or that they'll be seen as representing their entire race or ethnicity. When they do take the risk to share, the impact is profound—not just for them, but for the whole team.

The Culture of Silence and the Cost to Women of Colour

Most workplaces are set up to reward conformity, not candor. Women of colour who challenge the status quo are often labeled as "difficult" or "not a team player." The message is clear: keep your head down, especially if you're already underrepresented. This leads to self-editing, holding back, and missing out on the innovation and creativity that diverse voices bring.

What We Lose When Women of Colour Don't Feel Safe

When women of colour don't feel safe, organizations lose out on their best ideas, unique perspectives, and the kind of generative conflict that drives real progress. The cost is not just individual—it's collective. Silence becomes a habit, and organizations settle for mediocrity instead of excellence.

The Roots of Fear: Structural and Systemic Barriers

The fear experienced by women of colour is both human and structural. Many organizations are built on hierarchies that reward obedience and punish dissent. For women of colour, the threat of exclusion is compounded by the reality of being both a gender and racial minority—facing higher rates of discrimination, lower trust in reporting processes, and fewer opportunities for advancement.

Vulnerability as a Leadership Skill—And an Organizational Imperative

Teams that innovate are those where it's safe to disagree and to be wrong. Leaders must model vulnerability and actively create conditions where women of colour can speak up without fear. This means acknowledging and addressing both racism and sexism, and rewarding candor, not just compliance.

Designing for Safety: Practical Steps for Inclusion

Start meetings by inviting everyone, especially those from underrepresented groups, to share their perspectives.

Slow down and make space for quieter voices.

Name the elephant in the room: acknowledge when people are hesitant to speak up, and ask why.

Implement anti-racism and intersectional training, and collect intersectional data to inform targeted interventions.

Build networks of support and mentorship for women of colour, and ensure diverse representation in leadership pipelines.

The Cost of Silence: A Personal Reflection

For women of colour, staying silent is often a survival strategy. But the real tragedy is the missed opportunities—not just for individuals, but for teams and organizations. When psychological safety is lacking, everyone loses.

Building Psychological Safety for Women of Colour—One Step at a Time

Creating safety is a practice. It starts with acknowledging the unique challenges women of colour face, and committing to structural change. It means rewarding honesty, listening without judgment, and making sure every risk taken to speak up is met with respect and curiosity.

Pearls of Insight—With an Intersectional Focus

- ❖ **Psychological safety is foundational**, especially for women of colour who face compounded barriers.
- ❖ **Fear mutes potential**, and the cost is both individual and collective.
- ❖ **Skilled facilitation and inclusive leadership** can create the conditions for safety and belonging.
- ❖ **Breakthroughs happen when safety is present**—when women of colour are empowered to drop their guard and let themselves be seen.
- ❖ **The first step is to acknowledge the unspoken** and commit to intersectional change.

Your Turn: Reflect & Explore—Through the Lens of Women of Colour

1. On a scale of 1 to 10, how safe do women of colour feel to speak up or challenge the status quo in your workplace? What factors contribute to that number?
2. Can you recall a time when a woman of colour didn't share an idea or concern because it didn't feel safe? What happened next?
3. What's one small thing you could do today to foster safety for women of colour and others from marginalized backgrounds?

Creating psychological safety for women of colour isn't a luxury—it's the quiet revolution that unlocks not just their best work, but the best work of everyone

CHAPTER 12

Footprints in the Sand — Healing, Hope, and Finding My Voice

What if healing isn't about erasing pain, but about daring to keep walking with it? I used to believe that the only way forward was to "get over it"—to tie up old wounds and leave them behind. But life taught me otherwise: healing is a messy, unpredictable journey, marked not by perfection, but by every quiet step we take, even when the tide tries to erase our progress.

There's a quiet hope I hold, not just for myself, but for everyone carrying unseen burdens: one day, I hope you heal from the things you can't yet talk about. I hope you find peace in the places where pain still lingers. I hope those private aches and silent battles slowly fade, until they're no longer the first thing you think about in the morning or the last thing you feel before sleep.

But if there's one thing I've learned, it's that healing is rarely tidy or linear. It doesn't arrive on schedule, or stick to a clear progression. It can be slow, jagged, unpredictable. Sometimes it feels like you're making progress, only for an old wound to open again. Sometimes you stumble, fall back, and wonder if you'll ever really move forward. I've come to believe that maybe healing isn't a place you arrive, but a way you keep walking —

step by step, even when the sand is soft and the tide threatens to erase your tracks.

The Unspoken Things

For a long time, I thought the only way to heal was to "get over it." To leave the past behind, tie it up with a neat bow, and pretend the pain had vanished. But that's not how it works. Some hurts run too deep for simple fixes. Trauma, shame, loss — these things don't just evaporate because you will them away. They live in your body, in your nervous system, in the stories you tell yourself. Sometimes they're so overwhelming, you can't even put them into words.

I've carried my share of unspoken things. I grew up learning to keep secrets, to swallow my struggles, to show only the parts of myself that felt safe or acceptable. As a woman, as a person of color, as someone who thinks and feels differently from the "norm," I learned early that vulnerability could be dangerous. That sharing too much — or the wrong part of myself — might invite judgment, pity, or outright dismissal.

So I became an expert at hiding pain. I learned to soldier on, to keep moving, to succeed in spite of the weight I carried. Outwardly, I looked strong, capable, put-together. But inside, there were places I didn't dare go. Wounds I couldn't speak of. Hurts I thought I'd have to carry alone.

It's only recently, with distance and support and a lot of stumbling, that I've started to unlearn that lesson. That I've realized there's no shame in the things I can't yet talk about. That my worth isn't measured by how quickly I can "move on," but by my willingness to keep showing up — for myself, for others, for the messy, unfinished work of healing.

The Power of Footprints

Sometimes, when I feel stuck or lost, I imagine the beach at low tide. The sand is smooth, unbroken, until someone walks across it. Each footprint is a mark of presence, of movement, of someone who dared to keep going even when the path was unclear. The tide may come in and wash those prints away, but for a moment, they're there — proof that someone was here, that progress was made, that the journey mattered.

That's how I try to think about my own healing. I may not have all the answers. I may not be "healed" in the way I once imagined. But every time I choose to keep moving — to reach out, to reflect, to try again — I'm leaving a footprint. And maybe, just maybe, those footprints will help someone else find their way, too.

Because the truth is, we're never as alone as we think. For every silent struggle, there are countless others who've walked a similar road. And sometimes, the bravest thing we can do is leave a trace — a story, a gesture, a moment of honesty — for someone else to find.

Why Tell the Story at All?

There are days when writing about pain feels self-indulgent, or even dangerous. "Why me?" I wonder. "Why share this vulnerability, this messiness, when there's so much risk?" The world doesn't always reward those who open up. Sometimes it punishes them.

But then I remember something bigger: my story, for all its specificity, isn't just mine. It's part of a larger tapestry — one woven from the experiences of women, people of color, immigrants, neurodiverse folks, and so many others who move through the world with invisible burdens and unspoken dreams. Every time I speak honestly, I'm naming something that too often goes unnamed. I'm giving voice to realities that might otherwise stay hidden, validating the struggles and resilience of those who feel unseen.

Representation matters. When I was younger, I rarely saw anyone who looked or thought like me in positions of power, or even in the stories we told. The narratives that did exist were often filtered through someone else's lens — simplified, sanitized, or stereotyped. It's only by sharing the full range of our experiences, especially the hard parts, that we make space for others to do the same.

So I keep writing. I keep making footprints. Not because I have it all figured out, but because maybe the story of how I kept going can light a small candle for someone else. Maybe my struggles, reframed as lessons instead of failures, will become a chapter in someone else's survival guide.

Healing Is a Process, Not a Destination

If you're reading this and waiting for your pain to disappear, for your wounds to "heal" so you can move on, I want to tell you: you are not broken for taking your time. Healing is a process, not a finish line. There are days when you'll feel strong, and days when old hurts resurface. There will be moments of joy and moments of setback. That's all part of the work.

Progress, not perfection, is the goal. Every small act of self-compassion — taking a breath, asking for help, forgiving yourself for not being "over it" — is a step. The journey might be long, and it might not look like anyone else's. But each step matters.

Over the years, I've found that the most profound shifts come not from denying pain, but from making space for it. From honoring the parts of myself that still ache. From refusing to judge the pace of my own recovery. And from realizing that healing isn't just about me — it's about the community I build along the way.

Your Journey Is a Guidepost

There's a strange comfort in realizing that our struggles, while deeply personal, are also universal. The specific details may differ, but the feelings — shame, fear, loss, hope — are shared by so many. When you're in the thick of it, it's easy to believe you're alone. But every time someone else tells their story, a window cracks open. The world gets a little bit bigger, and the burden feels a little bit lighter.

Even if you're still struggling, your journey has value. Your resilience, your decision to keep moving, your willingness to try again — these are guideposts for others walking a similar path. You don't have to be fully "healed" to offer hope. Sometimes, the most powerful inspiration comes from those who are still in the process, still muddling through, still learning as they go.

If my footprints help someone else avoid a pitfall, or reassure them that it's okay to pause and rest, then sharing my story is worth it. If I can offer even a single practical insight — a coping strategy, a reminder to breathe, a glimmer of hope — then my pain is transformed into purpose.

Stories as Survival Guides

There's a quote I hold close: "One day you will tell your story of how you overcame what you are going through now, and it will become part of someone else's survival guide." That idea — that our pain can become someone else's map — is both humbling and empowering.

Stories create connection. They break isolation. They remind us that survival is possible, that healing is possible, that thriving is possible. When someone shares how they navigated a dark time, they offer more than advice — they offer proof. Proof that it's okay to struggle, to stumble, to not have all the answers. Proof that the journey is worth it, even when the destination is unclear.

For me, writing is both therapy and offering. It's a way to process what I've been through, and a way to give back. Sometimes, the act of putting pain into words is itself a step toward healing. Sometimes, the act of sharing those words is an act of hope — a message in a bottle, sent out in faith that it might reach someone who needs it.

Representation: Bearing Witness, Giving Voice

Being part of an underrepresented group adds another layer to this journey. I've often felt like I was moving through worlds not built for me — environments that didn't understand my background, my neurodiversity, my culture. The pressure to conform, to fit in, to mute the parts of myself that didn't match the mold, was relentless.

But I've also learned that my difference is my strength. My perspective, shaped by unique experiences, allows me to see things others might miss. And by speaking up, by writing honestly, I can help validate the experiences of others who feel similarly invisible.

Representation isn't just about being seen. It's about being understood, being valued, being heard. When I share my story — with all its nuance, struggle, and hope — I'm not just healing myself. I'm helping to build a world where others like me can find belonging.

Purpose Beyond Self

At some point, healing becomes about more than just personal well-being. It becomes about purpose — about using what you've learned to make a difference. For me, that means being a voice for those who can't yet speak, bearing witness to struggles that go unacknowledged, and offering hope to those who need it most.

Healing isn't about reaching a finish line—it's about making peace with your story, leaving footprints for others, and finding meaning in the journey itself. Even if you're still struggling, your willingness to keep moving becomes a guidepost for someone else searching for hope.

Pearls of Insight

- ❖ **Healing Is a Process, Not a Destination:** Progress, not perfection, is the goal. Be gentle with yourself. Some wounds may never fully disappear, but they don't have to define you.
- ❖ **Your Journey Is a Guidepost:** Even if you're still healing, your experience can offer hope and guidance to others. You don't have to be "finished" to be of service.
- ❖ **Stories Foster Connection and Survival:** Sharing your story of overcoming adversity transforms pain into a resource for others. Connection is the antidote to isolation.
- ❖ **Representation Matters: Telling your unique story** — especially as someone from an underrepresented group — helps validate and uplift others with similar experiences.
- ❖ **Purpose Beyond Self:** When you find meaning in using your voice for others, it can give you strength to persevere. Sometimes, sharing your story is the most generous thing you can do.

Your Turn: Reflect & Explore

1. **Unspoken Stories:** Without needing to share specifics, acknowledge within yourself if there are past hurts or challenges you don't yet feel ready to talk about. Offer yourself compassion for being exactly where you are in

that journey. Healing takes time, and it's okay to move at your own pace.
2. **Your Footprints:** What challenges have you already navigated? Even if you're not "fully healed," how might your experience offer insight or hope to someone facing something similar? Remember: your progress, however imperfect, can be a lifeline for others.
3. **Whose Voice?:** What groups or communities do you feel connected to or representative of? How might sharing aspects of your unique journey contribute to validating their experiences or fostering understanding? Maybe you're the first in your family to break a silence; maybe your story will make it easier for someone else to speak up.

As I learned to honor my own journey—messy, unfinished, and real—I realized that sharing my story could light the way for others. The next chapter asks: how do we transform our pain into purpose, and use our voices to build a world where everyone can belong?

PART III
FINDING VOICE, RECLAIMING POWER

CHAPTER 13
Don't Let Others Speak for Me

How many times have you swallowed your words, watching someone else narrate your story? For years, I was the quiet one in the room—nodding, listening, letting my ideas slip away or be claimed by louder voices. Each moment of silence felt small, but together, they became a pattern: I was giving away my power, one unspoken sentence at a time.

The Silent Cession: Reclaiming the Power I Gave Away

For most of my life, I let others speak for me. If you'd watched me in meetings or even at family dinners, you'd see someone nodding along, listening intently, but rarely raising my hand. I waited for a lull before daring to speak, only to have the moment slip away, or worse, be interrupted by a louder voice. When called on, sometimes I froze—mind blank, cheeks hot, certain that whatever I had to say would come out wrong. Why did I stay silent so often? The reasons blur together—a knot of shyness, anxiety, and the practiced habit of shrinking myself. Some days, it was fear of public speaking, the dread of putting my thoughts on display. Others, it was the fear of looking foolish, or worse, of being dismissed, ridiculed, or simply ignored.

But whatever the reason, the result was always the same: I gave away my power. Not in some grand, conscious act, but in a hundred small moments—by choosing silence, by letting someone else take the floor, by hoping someone would say what I couldn't. I waited for others to articulate my point, champion my cause, defend my perspective. I let others narrate my story, hoping—sometimes desperately—that they'd get it right.

It took me years to realize that this wasn't occasional. It was a pattern, deeply ingrained and almost invisible. It showed up everywhere: at work, in friendships, in my family, even in my own head. Every time I didn't speak up for myself, I was ceding my right to be heard. Every time I let someone interrupt or dominate a conversation, I was shrinking my space, my presence. Every time I avoided the literal or metaphorical stage, I was hiding my voice, my ideas, my expertise. Every time I wished someone else would fight my battles or call out an injustice on my behalf, I was outsourcing my agency.

For those of us who move through the world with marginalized identities, the stakes are even higher. The world is already structured to dim our voices—to speak over us, to define us, to tell our stories through someone else's lens. The cost of silence isn't just personal; it's systemic. And the luxury of passivity is one we can't afford.

The Pattern of Power Leaks

Letting others speak for me didn't feel like a choice at first—it felt like survival. There are real risks to speaking up, especially for those who carry the weight of stereotypes or expectations. I learned early that being "difficult," "loud," or "too opinionated" could come with consequences. Sometimes, it was easier (or safer) to just let things go.

But over time, those small acts of silence accumulated. Each one was a tiny leak in my sense of self. Each time I swallowed my words, I grew smaller, more hesitant. Each time I watched someone else shape my narrative, I felt myself drifting further from my own truth1.

Looking back, I can see how this pattern played out:

- ❖ **Meetings:** I'd have an idea, but talk myself out of sharing it. "Someone else will say it better," I'd think. And when someone else did, I'd feel a sting of regret—not just at being overlooked, but at not having claimed my own voice.
- ❖ **Interruptions:** If I was interrupted, I'd let it go, telling myself it wasn't worth making a fuss. But after a while, I started to notice a growing resentment—not just at the interrupter, but at myself for allowing it.
- ❖ **Opportunities:** When asked to present, to lead, or to step up, I'd shrink back, anxious about being exposed or making a mistake. I justified it as humility, but really, it was fear.
- ❖ **Advocacy:** When treated unfairly, I'd hope someone else would notice, would speak up, would defend me. Sometimes they did, but it rarely felt satisfying—because deep down, I knew I'd abandoned myself.

With time, two stark realizations hit me. First, these weren't rare lapses; they were daily habits. Second, in a world that already demanded more of me just to be heard, I couldn't afford to keep giving away my power. Agency isn't handed back—it's reclaimed, fought for, and protected, often at a cost.

The Allure of Excuses

Knowing this didn't make the habit easy to break. The excuses I gave myself were seductive, familiar, and often disguised as virtues:

- ❖ "I'm just tired. It takes so much energy to keep pushing."
- ❖ "I don't want to rock the boat or come across as negative."
- ❖ "I'm being a team player. I don't need the spotlight."
- ❖ "If it's important, someone else will say it."
- ❖ "It's just not worth the conflict or the discomfort."

But the more I interrogated these excuses, the more I saw them for what they were: justifications for staying small, for remaining complicit in my own disempowerment. Choosing comfort over assertion, appeasement over authenticity—these aren't acts of kindness; they're acts of abdication.

In truth, "niceness" can be a trap. We're taught, especially as women or marginalized people, that being agreeable is safer, more likable, less threatening. But when "niceness" means tolerating disrespect, swallowing injustice, or erasing your own needs, it stops being a virtue and becomes a form of self-betrayal.

The Moment of Reckoning: My Transformation Story

Let me share a story that crystallized this lesson for me—a turning point that changed how I show up in the world.

I was leading a massive transformation project and had delivered significant value to seven out of ten departments. However, I struggled with public speaking. Instead of presenting our achievements myself, I asked each department leader or spokesperson to share the impact I'd made. I thought I was being humble—giving others a platform and letting those positively affected tell their stories, rather than "blowing my own trumpet."

In reality, I was avoiding public speaking and shying away from owning the narrative. When the leaders presented, each did so in their own style, with their own stories. The result was chaotic—a collection of random anecdotes with no clear theme, message, or narrative. It was, as the feedback later put it, "a soup with too many cooks." And this happened in front of half the company.

The feedback was blunt: it was a poorly planned and executed presentation with no clear message. I was told I needed to "pull up my socks." This experience was a major setback in my career and for the transformation journey. By handing over the presentation, I had given away my power, my agency, and my story. I let myself down.

My manager—a supportive, inclusive, and empowering leader—gave me constructive feedback and even joined me in public speaking training. Determined to improve, I signed up for the next public speaking opportunity that came my way. Only after committing did I start working on my talk: developing the theme, the key message, and the narrative, eventually shaping it into a 15-minute TED-style speech. My team was incredible—they helped me refine my message, provided feedback, helped with the slides, and acted as my practice audience.

On the day of my first public speech, my manager, the Chief Information Officer, attended to support me. Friends from other companies also showed up. Just before I went on stage, another speaker delivered a talk very similar to mine. I had to quickly regroup, focus on being myself, and deliver my message. The presentation went really well. That day, I claimed my voice.

Since then, I've continued to sign up for public speaking opportunities, practicing and refining this skill again and again. I've spoken to audiences of 400 lawyers at a law conference and to groups as large as 800. It all started with a painful experience that I'll never forget—but it became the catalyst for my growth.

Agency Is Reclaimed, Not Given

Reclaiming agency isn't a single act—it's a practice. It means refusing to let others narrate your story, define your worth, or dictate your experience. It means learning to advocate for yourself, even when it's uncomfortable or imperfect.

For me, reclaiming my voice has meant:

- ❖ **Speaking Up, Even When Shaky:** I started with small moments—sharing an idea in a meeting, asking a question, stating a boundary. My hands would shake, my voice would wobble, but I did it anyway.
- ❖ **Interrupting the Interrupters:** When someone talks over me, I now say, "I'd like to finish," or "I wasn't done." It still feels awkward, but each time, it gets easier.
- ❖ **Taking Up Space:** I accept opportunities to present, to write, to lead—even when I doubt my readiness. Stepping onto the stage, literal or metaphorical, is terrifying, but I do it because shrinking serves no one.
- ❖ **Naming Injustice:** When treated unfairly, I try to speak up, whether it's about microaggressions, pay inequity, or dismissive behavior. I do it for myself, but also for others who might be watching.
- ❖ **Self-Advocacy as Self-Respect:** I remind myself that advocating for my needs isn't selfish—it's a form of self-respect. If I don't honor my own voice, why would anyone else?

Recognizing the Patterns

The first step to change is awareness. I started tracking the situations where I felt myself shrinking—who was in the room, what was being discussed, what fears bubbled up. I noticed patterns: I was more likely to stay silent around authority figures, in large groups, or when the topic felt personal. I'd hold back when I was tired, anxious, or doubting my expertise.

But I also noticed something else: the more I practiced speaking up, the easier it became. Each small act of self-advocacy built momentum. Each time I reclaimed my space, I felt a little stronger, a little more at home in my own skin1.

The Cumulative Effect of Small Acts

Power leaks don't happen in isolation. They add up, slowly eroding confidence and credibility. But the opposite is also true: small acts of reclaiming power accumulate, creating a new foundation of agency.

The first time I corrected someone who misrepresented my idea, my voice shook. The second time, it was easier. The third time, I didn't hesitate at all. Each boundary set, each opinion voiced, each moment of self-advocacy—they all add up. They become habits, and then, they become your default.

It's not about being loudest or most assertive. It's about being present, visible, and true to yourself. It's about refusing to disappear, even when it would be easier.

The Role of Support

Reclaiming agency doesn't mean doing everything alone. Along the way, I've learned the value of allies—people who notice when you're interrupted and redirect the conversation, who amplify your ideas, who encourage you to step up. I've learned to seek out spaces where my voice is valued, and to create those spaces for others.

But ultimately, no one else can claim your power for you. Allies can hold the door open, but you have to walk through it. You have to decide, moment by moment, to show up for yourself.

The Cost of Disappearing

The longer I stayed silent, the more I started to feel invisible—not just to others, but to myself. I lost touch with my own needs, desires, and convictions. I became a supporting character in my own life.

But the cost wasn't just internal. I missed out on opportunities, on connections, on growth. My ideas went unshared, my perspective unrecognized. I became complicit in my own erasure.

The world doesn't benefit from our silence. Every time we let others speak for us, we reinforce the structures that silence us. Every time we shrink, we make it harder for others to expand.

The Ongoing Journey

Reclaiming my voice is still a work in progress. Some days, I fall back into old patterns. Some days, the fear feels overwhelming. But now, I see those moments as opportunities—not failures, but invitations to try again.

I remind myself: agency is reclaimed, not given. My voice is my power. And every time I choose to speak, to assert, to take up space, I am writing a new story—for myself, and for others who are watching.

Refusing to let others speak for me has been a slow, sometimes painful, but ultimately liberating process. With every small act of self-advocacy, I am rewriting my story—proving, to myself and to others, that my voice is enough, and my story is mine to tell.

Pearls of Insight

- ❖ **Silence Is Abdication:** Failing to speak up for yourself, for any reason—fear, discomfort, habit—often equates to subconsciously giving away your personal power and agency.
- ❖ **Power Is Claimed, Not Given:** Especially for those facing systemic inequities, reclaiming power requires active effort, self-advocacy, and asserting your voice; it's rarely handed over freely.

- ❖ **"Niceness" Can Be a Trap:** Prioritizing being "nice" or avoiding conflict over asserting your needs or challenging unfairness can perpetuate your own disempowerment.
- ❖ **Recognize Your Patterns:** Becoming aware of the specific situations and ways in which you tend to give away your power is the first crucial step toward change.
- ❖ **Small Acts Accumulate:** Giving away power often happens in small, seemingly insignificant moments, but the cumulative effect can be profoundly disempowering. Conversely, small acts of reclaiming power build momentum.

Your Turn: Reflect & Explore

1. **Your Power Leaks:** In what specific situations or interactions do you notice yourself holding back, staying silent, or allowing others to speak for you or over you? What fears or discomforts typically underlie this? Take a moment to write down or reflect on a recent example.
2. **The "Nice" Trap:** Have you ever prioritized being "nice" or avoiding conflict over speaking up for yourself or something important? What was the outcome, both externally and for your own sense of self? How did it feel to remain silent, and what might you do differently next time?
3. **One Step to Reclaim:** What is one small, concrete action you could take this week to consciously reclaim your power in a situation where you might normally stay silent or defer? Maybe it's stating your opinion clearly in a meeting, setting a boundary with a friend, or correcting someone who interrupts. Commit to this action, and notice how it feels.

Reclaiming my voice was just the beginning. The next challenge: learning how to use it with courage, clarity, and compassion—even when the world pushes back.

CHAPTER 14
Owning My Worth—When Recognition Isn't Given

Sometimes, the moments that force us to confront our worth arrive not with fanfare, but with a quiet, simmering injustice. My story begins in a small fintech company—just twelve people, each of us hustling to carve out our place. I poured myself into my work, producing results I knew were worthy of recognition. But the culture of the company, shaped from the top down by the C-suite leader, had its own unspoken rules about who got seen, who got credit, and who was expected to quietly deliver in the background.

The Arrival of Jill—and the Familiar Pattern

It was around this time that our C-suite leader hired a new chief customer service officer, Jill. The title itself was curious—after all, we didn't actually have any customers yet. Jill was white, direct, and blunt, much like myself. Yet, when she gave me feedback, it was that I was "too direct and blunt." The irony wasn't lost on me. Jill and the C-suite leader bonded over a shared passion for cycling, and I quickly realized that my expertise and results were not the currency that mattered most in this environment.

As a contractor, I kept my head down and delivered excellent work, paid by the day, not as a permanent employee. I believed—naively, perhaps—that the work would speak for itself.

Recognition, Repackaged

Then came the "40 Under 40 Women in Finance" award—an opportunity for the company to shine. The C-suite leader decided to nominate Jill for this honor. When I saw the nomination materials, I was stunned: they described all the work I had done. The marketing lead wrote Jill's submission, Jill went for a professional photoshoot, had her hair and makeup done, and looked every bit the part of an award-winning executive.

Jill approached me, emotionless, and said, "I'm being nominated for the work you do. I feel bad." But I didn't see any real regret. I raised the issue with the C-suite leader, but they dismissed me, saying I was paid my day rate and what they did with my work was their prerogative.

The Cost of Being Overlooked

I was furious—angry, hurt, and jealous. I watched as a white man in the C-suite openly helped build the profile and brand of yet another white woman, while my own work and contributions were ignored. Everyone in the office saw what was happening, but they just shrugged. Some offered empty words, telling me to "chin up and move on." Others suggested I find a mentor or "godfather" to advocate for me.

This wasn't just about a missed award. It was about the pattern—the way organizations, especially those dominated by a tight-knit C-suite, decide whose work gets amplified and whose gets erased. It was about the hypocrisy gap: the difference between what companies say they value and what actually gets rewarded.

The Scarcity Trap and the Myth of Merit

For years, I'd believed in the meritocracy myth: that if I worked hard, delivered results, and stayed professional, recognition would follow. But the truth is, many workplaces operate on scarcity. There's an unspoken belief that there are only so many seats at the table, only so much light to go around. If you're not in the favored circle, your work is often used to bolster someone else's profile.

This is the cost of playing small, of waiting for validation from others. The system is designed to reward those who already have power and visibility, not those who quietly deliver. The lesson was harsh but clear: if I didn't claim my worth, no one else would.

Reclaiming My Worth

I confided in my best friend, who challenged me to reclaim my sense of self-worth. She told me to go to a trophy shop, buy myself a trophy, and put it on my desk as a reminder: my value isn't defined by external validation or awards given to others for my work. It felt silly and awkward, but I did it. That trophy still sits on my table—a symbol that I will never again outsource my self-worth. The system may be flawed, but I refuse to let it define me.

Living Your Values When the System Doesn't

This experience forced me to confront a deeper truth: values aren't what you say, they're what you do. The C-suite leader could talk about integrity and recognition all day, but when it came to action, the gap was glaring. The company's values were just words on a wall—what mattered was who you knew, not what you contributed.

I realized that I had a choice. I could continue to play small, hoping that someone would eventually notice my work, or I could claim my own worth, even if no one else did. I chose the latter. I stopped waiting for permission to be proud of what I'd accomplished.

The Power of Internal Validation

So much of playing small is about chasing external approval. If I keep everyone happy, if I don't rock the boat, maybe I'll finally feel safe. But the truth is, real safety comes from within. Self-worth isn't granted by others; it's something you claim for yourself, over and over. It's trusting that you are enough, even when no one else says so. It's remembering your value, even when the world would rather you forget.

Once you find that internal anchor, the urge to shrink starts to fade. You don't need to steal the spotlight, but you also don't need to run from it. You can simply stand in your truth, knowing that your power is both real and renewable.

When My Power Meets Yours

There's a myth that power is a zero-sum game: if I claim my worth, there's less for you. But real, grounded power multiplies. When I step into my light, I make it safer for others to do the same. When I refuse to shrink, I change the culture—little by little, voice by voice.

I've seen it happen: the first woman in a department to ask for a raise opens the door for others. The first person to call out a hypocrisy gap creates a safer space for everyone. We don't just rise alone. We rise together.

Practical Steps to Reclaiming Your Worth

This kind of change doesn't happen overnight. It's a process, full of slips and second-guessing. But here are some steps that helped me—and might help you, too:

- ❖ **Name the Diminishing Habits:** Notice when and where you play small. Is it in meetings? With certain people? Around particular topics? Write them down. Awareness is the first step to change.
- ❖ **Reflect on Your Achievements:** List your wins—big and small. Remind yourself that you earned your seat. You belong at the table. Your voice matters.
- ❖ **Take One Bold Action:** This week, pick a situation where you'd normally defer or shrink. State your opinion clearly. Volunteer for a project. Correct someone who misattributes your work. The first time is the hardest, but each time gets easier.
- ❖ **Celebrate Others:** When you see someone else stepping into their power, celebrate them. Say it out loud. Make space for their light. When we support each other, we all get braver.
- ❖ **Model the Change:** Remember: someone is always watching. Whether it's your kids, your colleagues, or a stranger in the room, your willingness to stand tall gives them permission to do the same1.

The Ripple Effect

Owning my worth changed everything, but it also brought new responsibilities. I learned that when I stand in my power, I create space for others to do the same. The world desperately needs more people willing to own their light—needs more voices, more courage, more authenticity. Needs you—not some smaller, safer version, but the real thing.

Every time you stand in your power, you make space for others to rise. When you honor your worth, you invite abundance—not just for yourself, but for everyone watching. Your playing small does not serve the world. And neither does mine.

Pearls of Insight

- ❖ **Acknowledge Your Worth:** Recognize the value you bring, based on your skills, experiences, and impact, rather than seeking constant external validation.
- ❖ **Playing Small Is a Disservice:** Diminishing your capabilities or holding back your voice serves neither you nor the world.
- ❖ **Authenticity Requires Courage:** Being true to yourself, especially when it challenges norms, is a courageous act that builds genuine self-worth.
- ❖ **Earned Place, Earned Voice:** Once you've earned your seat at the table, use your position and voice to advocate for positive change and the greater good.
- ❖ **Empowered People Empower Others:** Standing securely in your own power allows you to support and celebrate the power and success of others without feeling threatened.

Your Turn: Reflect & Explore

1. **Diminishing Habits:** In what ways might you subtly diminish your own worth or play small in professional or personal interactions? What triggers this behavior? Name it—that's the only way to change it.
2. **Owning Your Seat:** Reflect on your achievements and experiences. What evidence confirms that you have earned your place and your voice matters? Write it down. Let it be your anchor.
3. **Using Your Voice:** Identify one situation this week where you could consciously choose to use your voice more assertively or authentically, even if it feels slightly uncomfortable. What small step could you take? Commit—and then notice how it feels.

Owning My Worth—When Recognition Isn't Given

Owning my worth was the beginning. Next, I had to learn how to use my seat at the table—not just to claim space, but to create it for others, and to lead with courage even when the world pushes back

CHAPTER 15
Rewriting My Story

What if the most powerful thing you could do is rewrite the story you've always told about yourself? For years, I wore my scars as proof of what had been done to me—until I realized the real power was in taking the pen back, and choosing how the next chapter would read.

Rewriting My Scars: Owning My Voice, Transforming My Story

As I look toward the horizon—2025 and beyond—I find myself drawn again and again to a deceptively simple question: What story am I telling about my life? Is it a story of hardship and injustice, or one of grit and transformation? What thread deserves my focus now, as I weave together the strands of my ancestors' journeys, my own upbringing, and the future I want to create for myself and my children?

It's taken me years to realize that the story I tell myself isn't fixed. It isn't fate, or genetics, or the sum total of the things that happened to me. It's a living, breathing narrative—one I can edit, expand, flip upside down, or rewrite entirely. And the act of rewriting, of taking the pen back into my own hands, has been the most powerful shift of my life.

The Old Script: Wearing the Victim's Cloak

I didn't always know I was carrying a victim story. Most of us don't. It seeps in gradually, a drip-drip of self-pity, complaints, and quiet resignation. Why is this happening to me? When will it stop? When do I get my big break? When does life finally get easy? It's the soundtrack that plays on repeat during sleepless nights or those long walks when you can't shake the feeling everyone else got the easy road, and you're forever climbing uphill.

As women, the obstacles are thick, relentless, and often invisible to those not living them. There's the physical reality—managing periods, navigating pregnancy and childbirth right when your career is supposed to take off, the hormonal turbulence of perimenopause and menopause. And then there's the psychic load: entering the workforce starry-eyed, only to knock up against inequity, unconscious bias, passive aggression, microaggressions. You learn to expect less, to apologize more. You learn to make yourself smaller, to sidestep danger, to swallow your anger so it doesn't mark you as "difficult."

If you're a woman of color, the plot thickens. You're not just battling external prejudice but also the internal complexities of your own community—hierarchies, historical baggage, the leftover scripts from centuries of "knowing your place." For me, that meant carrying the unspoken weight of my Indian heritage, the caste system's shadow, and the everyday hypocrisies that shape how we see ourselves and each other.

All of this adds up. If you're not careful, it becomes the only story you know. A story of what's been done to you, what you've endured, how unfair it all is. A story where you are acted upon, instead of acting.

The Breaking Point: When the Old Story No Longer Fits

There comes a moment—sometimes in the middle of a crisis, sometimes in the hush that follows—when the old narrative just stops working. For me, it was less a lightning bolt than a slow, suffocating realization: the stories I was telling myself weren't inspiring me. They were keeping me stuck.

I'd wake up dreading another round of battles, expecting slights around every corner, bracing myself for the next disappointment. I told myself it was realism, maturity, "preparing for the worst." In truth, it was a kind of self-imposed prison. I was reinforcing the walls with every retelling. Each time I said, "Of course this always happens to me," I was cementing my own powerlessness.

Eventually, the weight became unbearable. I was tired of feeling like life was something happening to me, not something I was shaping. I was tired of waiting for things to get easier, for someone to notice and hand me the break I deserved. I wanted to feel—no, to know—that I could shape my own story, no matter what the past had been.

The Shift: From Victimhood to Gratitude

The turning point didn't come from a self-help book or a motivational seminar. It arrived in fragments—a quote here, a conversation there. "Life gives you equal amounts of challenge and support," someone said. It stuck with me. What if every hardship, every heartbreak, every "white angel" (as my Reiki healer calls them, referring even to those who hurt us) was sent to teach me something I needed to know?

That idea didn't erase the pain. It didn't excuse injustice. But it widened my perspective. It gave me permission to ask different questions: What did I learn from this? What resource did I discover in myself? Who showed up for me, even for a moment, when I needed it most?

Instead of tallying up only the injustices and slights, I began to see the moments of grace, the unexpected support, the inner strength that surfaced only when tested. I started to understand that gratitude is not about denying pain—it's about seeing the whole picture. About integrating both the shadows and the light.

Writing as a Tool for Transformation

This book is, at its core, an act of rewriting. Every word I put on the page is a decision to take ownership of my story. Writing has become my way of processing the swirling mess of emotions, untangling the knots of past experience, and searching for the wisdom hiding in the bruises.

There is a peculiar magic in naming things. When you write about pain, you shrink it to a manageable size. When you write about triumph, you let it echo louder than the doubts. When you write honestly—about the ugly, the beautiful, the mundane—you begin to see the threads connecting it all. You discover that you are not just a product of your circumstances, but the author of your interpretation.

And interpretation is everything. The same set of facts can be spun into a tragedy, a comedy, or a hero's journey. The power is in the telling.

The New Narrative: Resilience, Agency, and Compassion

Rewriting my story doesn't mean pretending the hard stuff never happened, or that I'm grateful for every injustice. It means refusing to let those moments define the limits of who I am. It means seeing myself as resilient, not broken; as a learner, not just a survivor.

I now choose to see myself as an active participant in my own life—a woman who can shape her path, even when the wind is against her. I look at the scars—not as evidence of defeat, but as proof of endurance and growth. Each one is a mark of a lesson learned, a challenge met, a resilience forged in the fire.

I've learned to hold space for both grief and gratitude. I can mourn what was lost or never given, while still celebrating what I've become. I can acknowledge the reality of bias and hardship, while also recognizing the allies, mentors, and moments of luck that carried me through.

Lessons from the "White Angels"

One of the most healing shifts for me has been reframing the roles of those who hurt me. My Reiki healer's words echo often in my mind: "Maybe God only sends white angels." Maybe every difficult person, every saboteur or critic, was sent for a reason—to teach me boundaries, to show me where I needed to heal, to push me to claim my voice more fiercely.

This isn't about excusing harm, but about reclaiming agency. When I see those people as teachers, not just tormentors, I can let go of bitterness. I can mine the experience for wisdom, not just wounds. Sometimes, the lesson is simply, "I never want to treat anyone the way I was treated." Sometimes, it's, "I need to stand up for myself, even when it's terrifying."

This lens doesn't erase the pain, but it softens its hold. It allows for understanding, if not always immediate forgiveness. It lets me move forward lighter, less burdened by old resentments.

Mastering the Internal War

The real war, I've come to realize, isn't out there. It's inside my own mind. The world will always be full of challenges—some fair, some unjust, some random. But the only thing I can truly control is my response: my thoughts, my emotions, the story I choose to tell about what happened.

Developing mastery over my internal narrative is a lifelong process. Some days, the old script sneaks back in: self-pity, blame, fear. But I catch it sooner now. I know I have the power to pause, to question, to rewrite.

Owning my voice starts here—not in boardrooms or rallies, but in the silence of my own mind. If I can change the story I tell myself, I can change everything.

Gratitude is my anchor. It's how I honor the past without letting it limit my future, how I see my scars as sources of strength, not shame. The story isn't finished yet—the pen is in my hand. This time, I'm writing the ending myself.

Pearls of Insight

- ❖ **Narrative is Power**: The stories we tell ourselves shape our reality. You can shift from a victim narrative to one of resilience and growth—at any time.
- ❖ **Challenges Shape Character**: Life's difficulties, while painful, contain the seeds of wisdom, strength, and compassion.
- ❖ **Acknowledge Both Shadow and Light**: True self-awareness means integrating both the hardship and the help, the scars and the support.
- ❖ **Writing as Transformation**: Putting your experiences into words is a powerful way to process, clarify, and reshape your internal narrative.
- ❖ **Internal Locus of Control**: While you can't always control what happens, you can learn to master your response—and find peace there.

Your Turn: Reflect & Explore

1. **Your Dominant Narrative:** When you reflect on the challenges in your life, what is the dominant story you tell yourself? Is it one of blame, victimhood, resilience, or learning? Is it serving you, or keeping you stuck?
2. **Shifting the Lens:** Think of a specific difficult experience. Can you find not only the pain, but also the support you received, the hidden strength you discovered, or the lesson that emerged?
3. **Taking Pen to Paper:** If you were to begin writing honestly about your own journey—even just for yourself—what's one story or scar you feel ready to explore and potentially reframe? What new insight might be waiting on the other side?

If rewriting my story gave me agency, the next lesson would be about how to help others see what's possible—sometimes not with words, but with a single, thousand-word picture.

CHAPTER 16
Drawing the Barriers— Visual Facilitation for Real Inclusion

A picture says a thousand words. I learned this not from a textbook, but in a room where words had lost their power. We were gathered—men and women—to talk about gender equity at work. The conversation started with good intentions, but quickly became a loop. The men nodded, said they understood, acknowledged the barriers, but always circled back to "fairness," "equal process," and "merit." The discussion spun in place—agreeing, disagreeing, but never moving forward. Language became a tool for exhaustion, a way to keep the problem unsolved and, inevitably, leave the women feeling defeated.

Frustration welled up. I stood, grabbed a marker, and drew a picture I'd seen before: a starting line. On the surface, it looked fair—everyone lined up, ready to run. But I began sketching the invisible barriers women face before they even reach that line. I drew how girls are raised to be accommodating, to pick up unpaid responsibilities—helping in the kitchen, caring for siblings—while boys are encouraged to be bold, to take risks, to fight for what they want. At the starting line, both may hold degrees, but the women carry invisible weights: not being taken seriously, lacking mentors, coaches, advocates, or sponsors—support that is so often handed to the men.

I drew the expectations: women making tea and coffee, taking meeting notes, cleaning up after workshops, smoothing over conflicts. Men, meanwhile, set audacious goals, build relationships, and walk away assuming someone else will make it all happen—supported by a network of "godfathers" who move them from sail to sail.

As I drew, other women joined in, adding their own barriers and metaphors—before and after the starting line. The men grew silent, their words suddenly powerless. The lack of diversity, equity, and inclusion was now visible on the wall—undeniable, inescapable.

That picture did what hours of conversation could not. It broke the cycle of polite debate and made the systemic barriers real. We needed that visual. We needed to see, not just hear, the unconscious bias and lack of equity and its impact on our community. The drawing landed the message in a way that words alone never could.

The Power of Visual Facilitation

This was the moment I truly understood the power of visual facilitation. In a world drowning in words—slides, reports, endless meetings—our brains crave clarity and meaning, not more data. Visuals cut through the noise. They make the abstract tangible and bring everyone into the conversation, regardless of their status or communication style.

When I began using visual facilitation in my work, I started with stick figures and simple diagrams. Over time, I learned methods like Bikablo, which helped me create clearer, more engaging visuals. But it was never about artistic skill. It was about making meaning visible, inviting every voice into the story, and unlocking solutions that words alone couldn't reach.

Visuals are levelers. The senior leader's jargon and the new hire's fresh perspective both find a place on the page. When people contribute to a shared picture—adding a note, drawing a line, suggesting a symbol—they feel seen. The image holds their voice. The solution becomes a mosaic, not a monologue. With each sketch, the group's collective intelligence grows.

Visuals and the Work of Inclusion

Inclusion isn't just about who is in the room—it's about whose voices shape the outcome. Visual facilitation gives everyone a tool to be heard, especially those who have been sidelined by traditional, word-heavy processes. In the story above, it wasn't just my drawing that shifted the conversation—it was the collective act of women adding their truths, making the invisible visible for all to see.

I've seen this play out in other settings, too. In Indigenous engagement work, for example, words were often used to dodge accountability. But a single image—showing the "accelerators" some enjoy and the barriers others face—made the truth undeniable. Visuals can force us to confront uncomfortable realities, bypassing the ambiguity of words and making empathy possible.

From Debate to Shared Understanding

Visual facilitation isn't about pretty pictures. It's about shifting from endless debate to shared understanding, from talking at each other to building something together. When I draw with a group, the act of co-creation is transformative. People see their ideas come to life, connect dots, and feel ownership of the outcome. Even the simplest sketch can anchor a complex discussion, serving as a living artifact—a shared story the team can return to again and again.

Visuals for Equity and Change

Diversity, equity, and inclusion work can't succeed if it stays trapped in polite conversation or buried under jargon. Real change demands that we make the invisible visible. Visual facilitation is a tool for that work. It helps us:

- ❖ **Clarify the real barriers:** Not just what's written in policies, but what's lived every day.
- ❖ **Invite every voice:** Drawing together lowers the barriers to participation.
- ❖ **Anchor change:** Visuals create shared memory—a reference point for future action.
- ❖ **Move from awareness to action:** Once the barriers are visible, it's harder to ignore them.

Pearls of Insight

- ❖ **Pictures Cut Through Complexity:** Visuals clarify, align, and make the abstract concrete—better than words alone.
- ❖ **Co-creation Fosters Ownership:** Drawing together builds buy-in and understanding.
- ❖ **Inclusion Is a Practice:** Visual facilitation gives everyone a way to participate, not just the loudest voices.
- ❖ **Visuals Anchor Change:** A shared image can keep a team focused and honest about what needs to change.
- ❖ **Empathy Through Seeing:** Pictures can force us to face uncomfortable truths and build empathy that words alone can't.

Your Turn: Reflect & Explore

1. **Try Visuals in Your Next Meeting:** When you sense a conversation going in circles, try drawing the issue. What do you see that wasn't obvious before?
2. **Map the Barriers:** Sketch out the visible and invisible barriers in your workplace or community. Who faces them? Who benefits from "accelerators"? What changes when you see it all at once?
3. **Invite Others to Add:** Don't draw alone. Invite others to add their perspectives. What new truths emerge when the picture is co-created?

As I embraced the power of visual facilitation, I realized that real inclusion and equity require more than talk. They demand that we see each other clearly—and that we're brave enough to draw what's really there. The thousand-word picture isn't just a tool for clarity; it's a catalyst for transformation.

CHAPTER 17
The Reciprocal Mirror

What if the greatest gift of mentoring isn't the wisdom you give, but the truths you discover about yourself? My first leap into mentoring wasn't planned—it was a collision of self-doubt and a call to action that forced me to ask: Who am I to guide anyone? But as I stepped up, I found that every piece of advice I offered was a message I needed to hear, too. Mentoring, I learned, is a mirror—reflecting growth in both directions

Mentoring: Fuel for Growth, Empathy, and Leadership Across Generations

Mentoring is an old idea, maybe as old as human civilization itself. In every culture, in every era, you'll find stories of the wise sharing with the young, of experience passing down the line. But the secret that gets missed—especially in the business world, where mentoring is often formalized and boxed in—is that mentoring is not a one-way street. It's a mirror, held up between two people, each reflecting something the other needs to see. Growth moves in both directions.

My Accidental Leap into Mentoring

My own formal mentoring journey started earlier than I ever expected. I was mid-career—not a newbie, but not a manager either. I felt like I was still figuring things out, still learning to navigate the weird, wonderful maze of modern work. Then I attended a women's leadership conference called "MAD: Make A Difference." Sam Collins, the force of nature behind it, stood on stage and declared her mission: to empower a million women by 2020, one mentor at a time.

Her call to action was electric, but my gut reaction was pure self-doubt. Who am I to be a mentor? I'm still learning. Why would anyone listen to me? I'm not even sure I have my own life together. The inner critic was loud, but there was a stronger pull underneath—a sense that it was time to give back, to pay forward what others had done for me. So, with equal parts terror and hope, I signed up.

I was paired with a young Indian woman, stuck in an admin job with the local police. She hated it, felt totally disconnected from anything she cared about. Over six months we met, talked, dreamed, made plans, and—slowly—things shifted. By the end, she'd landed a job on the prestigious Event Management team of the Royal Palaces in London. She was on fire, alive again. It wasn't just her career that changed; she found her confidence and, as a beautiful bonus, got engaged to her longtime partner during that time.

Every time I doubt my ability to help people, I remember her transformation. But what's less visible is how much I learned about myself in the process. Every nugget of advice I offered her, every bit of encouragement, turned out to be something I needed to hear, too. I'd leave our calls and scribble in my journal, realizing that the wisdom I shared was really a message to myself. Life, as it turns out, is a mirror. The things we say to others are often the truths we most need to face.

The Reciprocity of Mentoring

Over the years, I've been both a mentor and a mentee, formally and informally. The biggest surprise? Mentoring is never just about the "expert" guiding the "learner." It's about two people, each seeing themselves reflected in the other. The advice, encouragement, and insight flow both ways.

As I moved into more senior leadership roles, I became keenly aware of how easy it is to get stuck in your own assumptions. The higher you climb, the more you risk living in an echo chamber, surrounded by people who see the world as you do. Mentoring—especially with people outside your bubble—breaks that pattern.

I started assembling a portfolio of mentors, each with a different perspective. Some are further along the path, offering hard-won wisdom and a long view. Some are peers, walking beside me, facing similar challenges. And some are younger, forging new paths and questioning everything. They're the ones who see gaps and blind spots I miss, who remind me of the rebel energy I carried early in my own career.

When it works, mentoring isn't about hierarchy. It's about mutual respect, genuine curiosity, and the willingness to be changed by the encounter.

The Corporate Rebel: Eating Humble Pie

Early in my career, I wore the "corporate rebel" label with pride. I challenged policies, asked uncomfortable questions, and pushed for change—sometimes loudly, sometimes at my own expense. In London's investment banking world, I learned to keep my struggles hidden. You didn't admit to mental health challenges, or let on that you had a life outside work. You worked as if you had no family, no needs, no limits. Vulnerability was a liability.

Years later, as a leader myself, I found the tables turned. A young consultant on my team approached me, openly sharing their mental health struggles and frustrations with how things were done. Their honesty was bracing. For a moment, my old instincts kicked in—minimize, redirect, keep moving. But I caught myself. Here was someone doing what I never dared to do at their age: speaking truth, risking vulnerability. I realized how much I still had to learn.

Working with younger mentors is humbling. Their world is different: what my generation quietly endured, they question openly. Issues we considered unchangeable, they see as problems to be solved. It's uncomfortable at times, but it's also a gift. Their courage helps me become a more compassionate leader, one who brings everyone along on the journey—regardless of age, gender, race, or background.

Mentoring on Boards: The Long Game

My mentoring journey has also played out at the board level. These are not passive, ceremonial roles; they're hands-on, requiring real engagement and influence. Here, too, I seek mentors—often women and men of color who've navigated these spaces with authenticity and integrity. Their guidance has been invaluable as I step into new phases of my career.

Getting onto boards didn't happen overnight. I watched as men with "salt and pepper" hair were welcomed as wise elders, while women of a similar age faced ageism and bias. People see my board appointments now, but they don't see the years of groundwork—the long, slow climb, the 90% of the iceberg below the waterline.

My mentors helped me see the long view, to keep showing up even when progress felt glacial. Their support, and my commitment to paying it forward, has been central to whatever success I've found.

Key Advice for Mentors and Mentees

1. **To the Corporate Rebel:** Your energy and drive are powerful. Use them with compassion. Educate, guide, and build awareness—not just for yourself, but for those

you challenge. Remember, the people you're pushing are human, shaped by their own history.
2. **On Becoming a Mentor:** You'll never feel "ready." Don't wait for perfect wisdom or a flawless track record. Start where you are. Your messy, unfinished story is someone else's roadmap.
3. **Embrace Peer Mentoring:** The best relationships are peer-to-peer, regardless of age or title. You have as much to learn as you have to teach.

Building Your Mentoring Portfolio

Mentoring today isn't about finding one perfect guide. It's about building a "board of advisors" for your own life—a diverse set of people who each bring something different. Maybe you need career advice from someone in your industry, but creativity coaching from an artist, or life wisdom from a retiree. You're a unique product; your mentors should reflect that.

The best way to honor your mentors? Take action. Listening is nice, but implementing their advice—really wrestling with it, trying it on, even disagreeing thoughtfully—is a true sign of respect. Don't just collect advice like souvenirs; use it. Sometimes, the advice you need most is what you already know but aren't living. Come to the table with an empty cup, ready to be filled.

Pitfalls to Watch Out For

No relationship is perfect, and mentoring is no exception. A few patterns to avoid:

- ❖ **Lack of Punctuality/Commitment:** Respect your mentor's time. Don't flake.
- ❖ **No Follow-Through:** If you agree on actions or next steps, do them.

- ❖ **Exploitation:** Don't treat your mentor as a shortcut to endorsements or connections.
- ❖ **Not Paying It Forward:** The spirit of mentoring is generosity. Pass it on.

Mentoring should be transformative—a dance, not a transaction.

The Mirror Effect: Why Mentoring Works

Mentoring works because it's human. We learn best not from textbooks or training modules, but from stories and relationships. When someone believes in us, challenges us, and shares their experience, they give us permission to try, fail, and try again. And when we step into the mentor role, we see ourselves anew—our strengths and blind spots, our unhealed wounds, our unacknowledged wisdom.

The best mentors listen more than they talk. They don't rush to fix or advise; they ask questions, reflect back, and create space for growth. The best mentees are curious, open, and honest. They show up with humility, ready to learn.

But here's the secret: the lines blur. You'll find, again and again, that the roles swap—sometimes in a single conversation. One moment you're the wise guide; the next, you're the one being changed. Mentoring is a reciprocal mirror, and the reflections are always surprising.

Mentoring Across Generations: Learning Side by Side

Today's workplace is more multigenerational than ever. Boomers, Gen X, Millennials, Gen Z—all rubbing shoulders, each with their own worldview. The old model was "senior teaches junior." But that's changing. Younger professionals bring fresh ideas, challenge old assumptions, and aren't afraid to ask, "Why not?" Older colleagues offer perspective, resilience, and the context that only time can bring.

The richest mentoring happens when both parties are willing to learn. I've been mentored by people half my age—and have learned more than I ever expected. I've mentored people twice my age, and realized how much we share.

The Portfolio Approach

No one person has all the answers. In a world where careers (and lives) are more diverse and dynamic than ever, you need a mosaic of mentors. Seek out:

- ❖ Someone who's walked your path before.
- ❖ Someone walking beside you, living your current reality.
- ❖ Someone forging new trails—maybe younger, maybe from a different culture or background.

Let your "board of advisors" be as unique as you are.

When the Student Is Ready

There's a saying: "When the student is ready, the teacher appears." I used to roll my eyes at lines like that, but I've seen it come true. The right mentor shows up when you're open to growth. Sometimes it's a formal relationship; sometimes it's a passing conversation. The point is to stay curious, humble, and willing to be changed.

Paying It Forward

Mentoring is a gift. If someone has helped you, find a way to help someone else. It doesn't have to be grand. Sometimes a single conversation, a word of encouragement, or a shared lesson is enough to change a life's direction.

If you remember nothing else, remember this: mentoring isn't about having all the answers. It's about showing up—imperfectly, authentically—and being willing to share the journey. The wisdom you offer others will come back to you, reshaped and renewed. Growth is a gift you give and receive, again and again.

Pearls of Insight

- ❖ **Reciprocal Growth:** Both mentor and mentee grow. Insight flows both ways.
- ❖ **Embrace Imperfection:** You don't need to have it all figured out. Your struggles are valuable.
- ❖ **Diverse Mentorship is Key:** Seek out people who aren't like you, from different backgrounds, generations, and skillsets.
- ❖ **Action Honours the Mentor:** The best gratitude is thoughtful action.
- ❖ **Mentoring for Leadership:** Leaders who learn from younger generations become more empathetic, adaptable, and inclusive.

Your Turn: Reflect & Explore

1. **Your Mentoring Journey:** Think back. Have you ever mentored someone, formally or informally? Been mentored yourself? What sticks with you from those experiences? Was it the advice, or the sense of being seen?
2. **Identifying Your "Board of Advisors":** If you could assemble a personal board of mentors today, what mix of experience, background, and perspective would you want? Who's missing from your circle?

3. **Paying It Forward:** Mentoring doesn't have to be official. What's one way you could support someone this month? A word of encouragement, a connection, sharing a lesson learned—the small moments matter.

As I looked into the mirror of mentoring, I realized the journey of growth never truly ends. The next chapter would challenge me to carry these lessons forward—turning insight into action, and making a difference not just in one life, but across a community.

PART IV
BEHIND THE CURTAIN: INVISIBLE SYSTEMIC BARRIERS

CHAPTER 18
Unconscious Bias & Privilege

What if the roles you play in your family were written long before you were born? Growing up, I watched my sister become the golden child and my brother the unquestioned heir, while I—the quirky, angry middle child—couldn't help but notice the invisible rules shaping our lives. I saw the subtle ways bias and privilege played out, not just in the world outside, but around our own dinner table.

Growing up in our family was like living in a play where the script had already been written, and everyone knew their part—except me. My sister was the golden girl, and it wasn't just a nickname. She truly was remarkable: beauty, brains, discipline, focus, ambition—she was the whole package, and everyone knew it. Then there was my brother. In an Indian family, being the male child made him the center of gravity. His nickname was "Boss" because it was assumed, without question, that he'd run the family business one day. And then there was me: the classic middle child, quirky, angry, the one who didn't quite fit the mold.

From a young age, I saw it—the subtle, unspoken ways my parents favored my sister and brother. It wasn't malicious or intentional. It was unconscious bias, woven into the fabric of our family life. My parents didn't realize they were doing it. They were just following the script passed down to them by generations before. But I saw it. I felt it. I called it out. And for that, I was labeled the angry child, the troublemaker, the one who made things up. "It's all in your head," they'd say, dismissing my feelings as if they were nothing more than childish tantrums.

Even my sister and brother didn't get it. Why would they? They were on the receiving end of the privilege, basking in the attention and approval that seemed to come so effortlessly. When I tried to explain, they'd get defensive, even angry. "You're imagining things," they'd insist. My lived experience was denied, invalidated. The more they denied it, the angrier I became. It was a cycle that fed on itself.

The Other Side of Privilege

Years later, after I got married, I found myself on the other side of the privilege fence. My father-in-law became a second father to me. We shared long walks and even longer talks. He mentored me, nurtured my ambition, and coached me through some of the toughest moments of my life. He taught me how to read company reports with the mindset of a director and board member. He believed in me in a way that felt unconditional.

His own children and their partners were surprised by our bond. "He wasn't like that when we were growing up," they'd say. He lived with us on and off for ten years in London, and I realized, perhaps for the first time, what it felt like to be the favorite. I didn't have to fight for his attention or approval. I was seen, heard, and listened to—effortlessly. Even when he was in the ICU in India, I was the one he turned to for decisions. I knew I had his ear. I knew I was privileged. And this time, I didn't have to work for it. It was just given to me.

It was a strange experience, being aware of the unconscious bias in my favour. I saw how easy life could be when you're the one who's naturally supported, when doors open for you without you even having to knock. I had lived both sides of the story.

Privilege in the Workplace

Then there was another story—one that played out in the corporate world. I was working for a company that wanted to address unconscious bias and privilege in the workplace. HR brought in a hotshot consultant from big 4 consultancy to lead a session. But instead of the usual passive lecture, they opted for a workshop, hoping to make the message hit home.

We talked about the obvious biases—male versus female, but we also dug into ethnic and cultural diversity. As I facilitated the activity, two white privilege C-suite male leaders sat in the room, nodding along through the smooth talk and polished slides. But as soon as the real conversation started, the denials and objections came pouring out.

We discussed how women have to work twice as hard as men, and people of color have to work ten times harder. We talked about invisible barriers and unconscious bias. First came denial, then anger. Despite sharing real-life examples and scenarios, these leaders rejected the premise, pretended they had somewhere urgent to be, and walked out. Their exit was a statement to the rest of the group: "We don't support this diversity stuff."

I followed them out, knowing their actions spoke louder than words. They were angry, defensive, and only there because the board required it. As privileged older white men, they insisted they'd earned everything through hard work. "There are no invisible barriers, no unconscious bias, no privilege," they claimed. "It's all in your head. This is just how business is done."

They challenged me, saying this narrative made them out to be the villains. Their self-preservation instincts kicked in. I explained that unconscious bias doesn't mean you're a bad person—it starts with awareness and leads to corrective behavior. But they clung to the belief that the game was fair, that everyone had the same rules.

Both had wives—one who gave up her career to raise kids, the other who went part-time. In their industry, men stayed late, traveled for work, and made big decisions over drinks after hours. I told them, as a woman, I didn't have a wife at home to pick up the slack. I missed out on those after-hours conversations and decisions. They shrugged. "Other women do it. If you want the job, you play the game. We're not changing it for you."

As a woman with kids, I struggled. The women would joke: "Either you don't have a husband and kids, or you have an extra wife at home to handle it all while you play the big boys' game." The system wasn't built for us.

The Illusion of Progress

I'm glad diversity, equity, and inclusion (DEI) have become topics of conversation. But in many organizations, it's still just a tick-box exercise—some training, a few activities, and then back to business as usual. Some companies set quotas for women in leadership, but often it feels like they're set up to fail, as if to prove that diversity doesn't work. Even now, unpublished reports show women earn 25% less than men. Nobody even bothers to look into the disparities for women of colour or people of colour. Most companies get stuck on the definition of "person of colour," never mind addressing the deeper issues.

There's a rush to address other marginalized groups—LGBTQ+, Indigenous, neurodiverse—but when I bring up women of colour, or people of colour, the conversation stalls. As women of colour, we're lumped in with all women. Men of colour are ignored entirely.

I was once asked, "Maybe this is just how it is in every society when you're a minority. Shouldn't you just accept it?" No. I refuse to accept the stereotype or the status quo. Awareness is the first step, but it's not enough. We need action, accountability, and real change.

Awareness is only the first step. Real change demands more than ticking boxes or having tough conversations—it means challenging the scripts we inherit, holding ourselves and others accountable, and refusing to accept the status quo. I will not let my story, or anyone else's, be defined by someone else's comfort with inequality.

Pearls of Insight

- ❖ **Unconscious Bias is Real—Even When We Can't See It:** Most bias isn't intentional. It's woven into our upbringing, our workplaces, and our everyday interactions. The first step is acknowledging it exists—even if it makes us uncomfortable.
- ❖ **Privilege is Invisible to Those Who Have It:** When you're favoured, it feels normal. You don't see the extra support, the open doors, the benefit of the doubt. But for those without it, the difference is glaring.
- ❖ **Denial is a Defence Mechanism:** When confronted with privilege or bias, many people react with denial or anger. It threatens their self-image and sense of fairness. Real change requires moving past denial to honest reflection.
- ❖ **Lived Experience Matters:** If someone tells you they feel excluded or discriminated against, believe them. Dismissing their reality only deepens the wound.
- ❖ **Tick-Box Diversity Isn't Enough:** True inclusion means more than quotas and workshops. It requires a shift in culture, ongoing accountability, and a willingness to change the rules of the game.
- ❖ **Intersectionality is Often Ignored:** Women of colour, men of colour, and other minorities are frequently overlooked in diversity efforts. One-size-fits-all solutions don't work for everyone.

Your Turn: Reflect and Explore

Take a moment to reflect on your own experiences with unconscious bias and privilege. Use these prompts to guide your thoughts or journaling:

1. **When have you felt unconsciously favoured or overlooked?** How did it shape your confidence, opportunities, or relationships?
2. **Have you ever dismissed someone's experience of bias?** What made you react that way? How might you respond differently now?
3. **Where do you see privilege operating in your family, workplace, or community?** What are the subtle signals or unspoken rules?
4. **If you have privilege, how can you use it to support others?** If you lack privilege, how do you advocate for yourself and others?
5. **What would real inclusion look like for you?** What changes would make you feel truly seen, heard, and valued?
6. **Who are the voices missing from your table?** How can you invite them in and learn from their stories?

As I moved from awareness to action, I realized that breaking cycles of bias and privilege isn't just about calling out what's wrong—it's about building new systems, new stories, and new ways of leading that truly include everyone.

CHAPTER 19
Beyond the Posters—Living Your Values

You can spot them in every corporate office: glossy posters shouting "Integrity," "Collaboration," and "Respect." But what happens when those values are just wallpaper—recited, displayed, and utterly ignored when it matters most? My first client in the mining sector taught me that the real test of values isn't what's printed on the wall, but what happens when power, ego, and pressure collide behind closed doors

I should have seen the warning signs.

When Values Become Wallpaper

When I launched my business, I imagined spending my days helping clients untangle complex ideas and transform them into focused products ready for market. My first client was a supplier in the mining, oil, and gas sector—an industry notorious for its tough culture—but I figured, how challenging could it really be?

The brief seemed straightforward: clarify their jumbled concepts into a digital product they could actually launch in the market. I worked with one main contact, and we'd meticulously planned the approach, agreed on scope, and set a twelve-week timeline. Everything looked perfect on paper, neat and organized like those values posters adorning their walls.

Until I walked through their doors.

From the very first week, I found myself living in a blueprint for what happens when company values exist purely as decoration. The scope shifted daily like sand in the wind, office politics bubbled constantly just beneath the surface, and the "alignment" we'd carefully negotiated proved to be nothing more than a mirage. They had budget for ten weeks, but the work required was easily double that timeline. My contact—the person who had brought me in and vouched for the project—walked out of his own meeting at the first sign of internal pressure, leaving me stranded in a room with two senior leaders, one of them from the C-suite.

During what was supposed to be a collaborative workshop, with all stakeholders focused on reviewing our timeline, everything went sideways. Instead of working together to solve problems, they systematically challenged every step and decision I made on the approach and timeline. This wasn't the kind of productive challenge that sharpens thinking and improves outcomes. This was something entirely different—the kind of aggressive questioning designed to corner, diminish, and establish dominance.

I was the expert they had hired, with a proven process that I knew worked. Meanwhile, they had been spinning their wheels on this same product for three years with nothing to show for it. But ego and bravado took control of the room. They hammered away at my recommendations, heckling my expertise, insisting they knew better, making it crystal clear that I was an outsider in this industry. What started as a "spirited discussion" quickly devolved into plain intimidation—the kind that feeds on making someone else look small and powerless.

The most disturbing part? They were enjoying themselves. They actually settled back in their chairs, trading those knowing side-glances that said they were congratulating themselves on a job well done—at my expense.

The Moment of Truth

I maintained my professionalism as long as humanly possible, explaining concepts, educating them on industry best practices, desperately trying to redirect the conversation back to the actual work. But after an hour of this treatment, clarity struck like lightning: this wasn't a debate about methodology or timelines. This was a power game, and the sole objective was to break me down piece by piece.

I stopped them mid-sentence. With my voice steady but my entire body shaking inside, I told them their behavior was completely unacceptable. I was upset, I announced, and I was going for a walk. When I returned, I would give them my decision about how to proceed.

The shock on their faces was palpable. You could literally see the moment someone yanked the plug on their entertainment.

Outside, I circled the block twice, jacket zipped tight against the wind, trying to calm the storm raging in my head. When I started this company, I had made myself a solemn promise: I would be the kind of leader I wanted to see in the world. I would hire consultants, not doormats. I wouldn't accept this treatment for myself or anyone on my team. If I allowed this behavior at the very beginning, what message would that send for every project that followed?

I called my husband, my voice tight with emotion. "It's my first client," I said, "but I think I have to walk away." His response was immediate and unwavering: "If they're treating you like this now, what will it be like later?"

That conversation gave me the courage I needed.

Drawing the Line

I walked back into that building with purpose. I asked to speak directly with the C-suite leader. Looking him in the eye, I delivered my message with absolute clarity: "I will not be bullied, intimidated, or harassed. If you're so confident you know better than the expert you hired, you can solve this problem yourselves."

He tried to minimize what had happened, dismissing it as "just how things work in this industry" and calling it a simple "project management discussion." I cut through his deflection immediately. What I had experienced wasn't a discussion—it was bullying, plain and simple. I told him I expected to be paid for the work I had completed, and then I would leave. I pointed out the internal misalignment and toxic politics that had made me a scapegoat for leadership dysfunction that had nothing to do with me.

"You're the leader," I said firmly. "It's your job to fix this culture, not use me as a punching bag for your team's frustrations."

Something in my directness must have penetrated his corporate armor. He apologized sincerely and said he didn't want me to leave. We established new ground rules for working together: it would be his responsibility to intervene when conversations turned toxic. I made it clear that when discussions crossed the line from constructive disagreement to undermining conflict, I would call him in, and he would handle it immediately.

I had to call him in more than once during that project.

The Values Facade

The company culture didn't magically transform overnight. Every time I called out inappropriate behavior, they became angrier, like children whose favorite toy had been confiscated. They had grown comfortable with their power dynamics—this intoxicating rush that came from dominating others in meetings.

Everywhere I looked, those values posters mocked the reality of daily operations—plastered on walls, stuck to conference tables, displayed prominently in reception areas. When I finally called them out directly, pointing to the disconnect between their stated values and actual behavior, they laughed. They actually laughed and told me the posters were purely for show, designed to help them win tenders and look good to clients.

"Nobody in this industry actually lives these values," they explained with cynical amusement. "It's all smoke and mirrors. You just have to roll with it to survive in this business."

But I didn't roll with it. In their world, that refusal was shocking—especially coming from a woman in a male-dominated environment. They tested me repeatedly, pushing boundaries to see if I would eventually cave to their pressure. Each time, I called it out. Maybe I didn't single-handedly transform their entire corporate culture, but I fundamentally changed how they treated me. And in a world where small victories often lead to larger transformations, that absolutely counts.

Understanding the Values Gap

This experience taught me something profound about the chasm between stated values and lived values. Most organizations aren't deliberately lying when they craft those inspiring statements. Leadership teams invest real time and significant money trying to capture the essence of their culture in a handful of carefully chosen words. There are facilitated workshops, mountains of sticky notes, and sometimes expensive consultants. Leaders genuinely talk about "walking the talk," and initially, people make sincere efforts to embody these ideals.

But culture is remarkably stubborn. It's not defined by what people wish they did or intend to do. Culture is what people actually do, especially when no one is watching or when pressure mounts.

When deadlines loom ominously, when major clients threaten to walk away, when someone makes a costly mistake—that's when authentic values surface. Sometimes they align perfectly with those polished posters. More often, they reveal an entirely different set of operating principles.

Values as Action, Not Decoration

Here's the fundamental truth I've discovered: values aren't nouns hanging static on conference room walls. They're verbs—active, dynamic forces that only matter when you actively practice them. They must show up consistently in your choices, your conversations, and your willingness to do what's right, especially when it's difficult or costly.

Integrity isn't a decorative word on corporate wallpaper. It's saying no to a lucrative deal that crosses ethical lines, even when everyone desperately wants to close it. It's providing honest feedback when staying silent would be easier and more comfortable. It's aligning your words with your actions repeatedly, even when no one is monitoring your behaviour.

Many organizations fall into what I call "values washing"—their posters look professionally designed, their websites are perfectly polished, but underneath lurks a gap that feels like organizational rot. Employees sense this disconnect immediately. When there's a wide chasm between what's proclaimed and what's practiced, trust erodes systematically, engagement plummets, and cynicism spreads like a virus. Sometimes this outcome is worse than never discussing values at all.

Recognizing Real Culture

Want to understand an organization's authentic values? Don't study the poster collection. Examine what gets rewarded. Who receives promotions, and who gets quietly sidelined? Which behaviours are tolerated—sometimes even celebrated—despite contradicting stated values?

Organizational culture emerges from accumulated stories: what happened last time, and the time before that, and the patterns that establish themselves over months and years. If people observe that corner-cutting leads to advancement, they'll cut corners too. If mistakes result in harsh punishment, they'll hide problems rather than solve them. If only certain demographics consistently rise to leadership positions, diversity and inclusion posters become cruel jokes.

Personal Values Experiments

This tension between stated and lived values isn't merely an organizational challenge—it's deeply personal. I regularly ask clients and myself: what are your authentic core values? What lines will you absolutely refuse to cross, regardless of pressure or consequences?

I conducted a personal experiment that proved illuminating. I identified three core values and made them my decision-making compass for an entire week. Every choice, every interaction, every response was filtered through those value lenses. The result surprised me: I moved more slowly through my days. Old habits—like reflexively saying yes to every request—became much harder to justify when measured against my stated principles. But I felt more authentically myself, less like I was running someone else's predetermined race.

The Courage to Live Authentically

Living your values rarely manifests as dramatic, movie-worthy moments. It's typically incremental, sometimes invisible, and often uncomfortable. It means initiating difficult conversations instead of avoiding confrontation. It means calling out behaviour that contradicts stated principles, even when doing so feels risky. It means modelling the change you want to see, even when you're exhausted or outnumbered.

I remember serving on a board where "respect" was prominently featured as their primary value. Yet meeting after meeting, the loudest voices consistently steamrolled quieter members. The path of least resistance would have been ignoring this pattern. Instead, I began inviting quieter members to speak first and gently redirecting interruptions when they occurred. It wasn't revolutionary, but the culture gradually shifted. People noticed these small changes. That respect poster slowly began representing something real rather than aspirational.

Practical Steps Forward

How do you bridge the gap between laminated ideals and daily reality? Start with these concrete actions:

Model the Values Personally: Leaders must walk their talk consistently. If you want honesty in your organization, be honest—especially when it's painful or inconvenient.

Build Genuine Accountability: When someone acts outside stated values, there must be meaningful consequences. Silence becomes complicity, and complicity erodes credibility.

Tell Authentic Stories: Celebrate specific moments when values are lived courageously. Use real stories to teach, reinforce, and inspire others to follow similar paths.

Make Culture Everyone's Responsibility: Organizational culture isn't owned exclusively by HR departments or executive teams. It's created daily by every single person through countless small decisions.

Embracing the Difficulty

Let's be completely honest: living your values is hard work, especially in organizations where speed dominates everything else. The shortcut always beckons seductively—close the deal regardless of ethics, hit the numbers at any cost, keep your head down to avoid conflict. But every time you choose the easy path, you make a fundamental choice about who you are and what you truly stand for.

I worked with a client who, under intense pressure to hit monthly targets, was offered a "creative" accounting solution. It would have made their numbers look fantastic and relieved immediate pressure. It also would have violated every value the company claimed to hold sacred. She paused, recognized the ethical conflict, and refused to participate. The month's numbers looked disappointing, and the pressure from leadership was very real. But the respect she earned from her team and herself proved lasting and valuable.

Personal Alignment as Foundation

You cannot control entire organizational cultures single-handedly. But you maintain complete control over your own choices and behaviour. You can choose to align your actions with your values consistently, even when it feels slow, even when it's challenging, even when others pressure you to compromise.

This is how cultures truly change—from the inside out, one principled decision at a time. When you live your values authentically, you give others permission to do the same. You become a living invitation for courage, honesty, and work that feels meaningful rather than hollow.

Living your values is rarely dramatic. It's the daily, often invisible, choice to align words and actions—especially when it's uncomfortable, costly, or slow. The posters may fade, but the culture you choose to embody will outlast any slogan

Pearls of Insight

- ❖ **Values Are Verbs, Not Nouns**: True values exist in daily actions and decisions, not just in decorative statements on walls.
- ❖ **The Gap Between Stated and Lived Values Destroys Trust**: When words and actions consistently misalign, organizational credibility evaporates.
- ❖ **Culture Reveals Itself Under Pressure**: Real values surface when stakes are high and comfortable choices aren't available.

- **Personal Alignment Creates Ripple Effects**: When you courageously live your values, you inspire others to examine and live theirs.
- **Small Consistent Actions Create Cultural Change**: Revolutionary transformation happens through accumulated small choices, not dramatic gestures.

Your Turn: Reflect and Explore

1. **Examine Your Organization's Values**: What values does your workplace claim to hold? How well do daily behaviours and decisions align with these stated principles?
2. **Identify Your Core Values**: List three to five values that matter most to you personally. How do they show up in your work and relationships?
3. **Spot the Gaps**: Where do you see disconnects between what people say they value and how they actually behave?
4. **Choose One Action**: Select one value you want to live more fully this week. What specific action can you take to embody it?
5. **Build Your Courage**: When have you compromised your values for convenience or pressure? What would you do differently now?

As I learned to bridge the gap between stated ideals and lived reality, I realized the next step was even harder: cultivating the courage to lead change from the inside out, one principled decision at a time.

CHAPTER 20
Never the Right Time

There's never a right time for women to have babies—only a brutal truth you discover when you're forced to choose between ambition and motherhood. The world tells you to plan, to wait, to find the perfect moment, but that moment never comes. Instead, you stand at the crossroads, juggling dreams and diapers, and realize the system was never designed for you to win at both.

The timing is always wrong. Too early in your career, and you're told you haven't proven yourself yet. Wait until you're established, and suddenly you're too old, the biological clock is ticking, fertility becomes a concern. There's this mythical sweet spot that everyone talks about but no one can quite define—that perfect moment when you've achieved enough professionally to take a step back, but not so much that you're indispensable. Spoiler alert: that moment doesn't exist.

What exists instead is a system designed to penalize women for the audacity of wanting both professional fulfillment and a family. A system that whispers, "Choose one," while pretending to offer support for both.

Early Lessons from the Slow Lane

Very early in my career, back in the relentless, testosterone-fueled world of investment banking, I witnessed what would become a defining lesson about motherhood and ambition. I watched a colleague return from maternity leave, and her story haunted me for years.

She had been a force of nature before her baby—ambitious, driven, the kind of person who lit up when she talked about complex deals and market strategies. She was the one who stayed late to perfect presentations, who volunteered for the toughest clients, who seemed destined for leadership. But after her baby, something shifted. She asked to switch to part-time—three days a week. It seemed reasonable. She worked in an all-female team, so you'd think she'd find understanding, maybe even advocacy.

Instead, I watched something insidious unfold.

Because she wanted to work part-time, and because she mentioned her children often—little comments about daycare pickup times, stories about first steps, the occasional phone call about a sick kid—a perception quietly developed that she was no longer "serious" about her career. Managers began to whisper that she wouldn't give 100%, that she was "distracted," that she'd lost her edge.

The high-stakes projects, the ones that required travel or unpredictable hours, gradually stopped coming her way. Instead, she was given the administrative work, the routine tasks, the safe, boring assignments that nobody else wanted. When she asked for more challenging work, for the high-profile assignments that could advance her career, she was told no—they needed someone full-time, someone who could "really commit" to the demanding hours.

I watched her transformation with a sick feeling in my stomach. What had once been passion became resignation. She stopped volunteering for anything extra. She stopped contributing in brainstorming sessions with the same enthusiasm. The woman who used to arrive early and leave late now came in precisely at 9 and left exactly at 5, because that's what they expected of a "part-time worker."

She was effectively moved to the slow lane, watching helplessly as friends and colleagues—many with less talent and experience—overtook her in the fast lane. She tried desperately to prove herself through the mundane projects they gave her, working with meticulous attention to detail, hoping someone would notice her value. But the door to advancement had already closed, quietly and without ceremony.

The last I saw of her, she was heading off on maternity leave for her second child. I often wonder if she ever came back. Sometimes, what looks like care and support—"We're being understanding about her family situation"—is just another way to sideline women. She would have thrived on those high-profile projects. Her skills hadn't diminished; only others' perception of her value had.

My Own Story: The Unexpected Gatekeepers

When I had my first child, I was determined not to become another cautionary tale. I had watched what happened to women who "leaned out," and I was going to lean in harder than ever. Once my baby settled into a routine, once I understood her patterns and needs, I reached out to my team and offered to do testing for a project I knew inside and out—one where I had written many of the requirements and understood the system better than anyone.

The project manager, a man was enthusiastic. "That would be fantastic," he said. "You know this system better than anyone." Even the CEO, when consulted, gave his approval. It seemed like a perfect arrangement—I could contribute meaningfully while maintaining the flexibility I needed as a new mother.

But the final decision rested with the program manager, and this is where my story takes an unexpected turn. She was a woman—highly competent, well-respected, someone I had admired and hoped would be an ally. She had never had children, had built her career through sheer determination and long hours, and when I presented my proposal, her response was swift and final: absolutely not.

"Unless you can come into the office every day and test the system under my direct supervision, I can't approve this," she said. Her reasoning? She assumed I would be distracted, that my baby would cry all day and I wouldn't be able to concentrate, that I would "take advantage" of the remote work arrangement.

The irony was crushing. Testing was perhaps the most visible, transparent job in the entire software development project. Every bug found, every test case completed, every piece of functionality verified was documented in real-time. It was impossible to slack off because your productivity was measured and visible to the entire team every single day.

But her mind was made up. In her view, mothers couldn't be trusted to work unsupervised. She had bought into the same stereotypes that kept women from advancing, and now she was gatekeeping other women's opportunities.

That was my first harsh lesson about workplace dynamics after motherhood: sometimes, the people you expect to be your allies are your biggest obstacles. Sometimes, women who have never walked your path are the least sympathetic to your struggles.

Career Suicide and the Unspoken Rules

As my first child grew older and I began to think about long-term career planning, I had lunch with a executive director I respected enormously—an incredible French woman who had somehow managed to climb to the executive level while raising three children. She was my role model, proof that it could be done.

Over wine and salad, I confided my thoughts about work-life balance. "I'm thinking about asking to go to four days a week," I said. "Just one day less, to spend a bit more time with my daughter."

Her reaction was immediate and serious. She put down her fork and looked at me with an intensity that made me uncomfortable. "Even having this conversation is career suicide," she said quietly. "You never, ever talk about wanting to work less. You work like you don't have babies."

I was stunned. This was a woman I admired, someone who seemed to have it all figured out. "But how do you manage it all?" I asked.

Her answer was revealing and devastating in equal measure. "I have a full-time, live-in nanny and a husband who has completely prioritized my career over his own," she said. "And even then, we never, ever speak about our children at work. That's the price of admission."

The unspoken rule was crystal clear: motherhood could not be visible in the workplace. You could be a mother, but you had to be invisible about it. You had to work as if you had a wife at home handling everything, just like your male colleagues did.

Second Chances and Strategic Navigation

When I had my second child, I genuinely thought my career was over. Two kids, the demands of motherhood doubling, the logistics becoming exponentially more complex—how could I possibly maintain the level of performance and commitment that leadership roles required?

But then, something unexpected happened. One of my previous managers, someone who had witnessed my work and capabilities firsthand, reached out with an opportunity that seemed impossible. He wanted me to lead a massive innovation program. The scope was enormous, the visibility high, the potential impact significant. My baby was only four and a half months old.

"I know the timing isn't ideal," he said, "but I've seen what you can do. I don't believe having kids changes your capabilities."

I was so grateful I nearly cried. Here was someone who saw my potential rather than my limitations, who understood that becoming a mother had made me more efficient, more focused, more strategic—not less capable.

From that experience, I learned to be incredibly strategic about my career choices. I had always been ambitious, but now I understood that I couldn't afford to waste time on roles that wouldn't advance my trajectory. I learned early that good girls don't get the corner office—you have to actively pursue the high-profile, challenging projects and make sure you deliver exceptional results.

After witnessing what happened to my colleague who got sidelined into boring work, I became acutely aware of the importance of positioning myself on strategic, visible projects. Some assignments seemed mundane on the surface, but I would dig deep to understand their significance, their broader impact, their connection to organizational priorities. That's what kept my interest and passion alive, even when the work itself wasn't inherently exciting.

I systematically avoided low-profile, routine roles—not out of arrogance or entitlement, but because I understood the critical importance of brand, reputation, and visibility in career advancement. Once you get stuck in the slow lane, it becomes exponentially harder to fight your way back to the fast lane. I had seen too many talented women lose their momentum and never recover it.

The Motherhood Efficiency Paradox

The stakes were higher than ever, the pressure relentless, but somehow I delivered better work than I ever had—even with babies, sleepless nights, and the constant mental load of motherhood. Investment banking had always demanded brutally long hours, and before children, I had worn those hours like a badge of honour, staying until midnight to perfect a model or sitting through endless meetings that could have been emails.

But after kids, I became clockwork: 8 AM to 5 PM, laser-focused, ruthlessly efficient. There was no time for office politics, no bandwidth for idle chatter or unnecessary meetings. I did more meaningful work, and consistently better work, in those compressed hours than I had ever accomplished in my previous twelve-hour days.

I established a non-negotiable rule: I leave by 5 PM, no exceptions. If someone attempted to schedule a meeting after 5, I would ask for a reschedule or decline outright. I expected pushback, resistance, maybe even career consequences. Instead, something interesting happened.

Because my current project was high priority and my results were consistently strong, very senior managers began to respect my boundaries. They worked around my schedule rather than demanding I work around theirs. Even I surprised myself with the confidence to say no, to ask for what I needed, and to stick to those boundaries without compromise.

The efficiency paradox of motherhood is real: when you have less time, you become ruthlessly prioritized about how you spend it. The mother who leaves at 5 PM often accomplishes more in eight hours than her childless colleague does in ten, because she can't afford to waste a single minute.

The Systemic Issues We Don't Discuss

But let's be honest about the cost. There's a silent, invisible tax that women pay for having children—a tax that goes far beyond the obvious financial implications of childcare and reduced income during maternity leave.

It's the opportunities that never come your way because you're perceived as less committed. It's the projects you're not offered because they require travel or unpredictable hours. It's the after-work networking events you miss because you have to pick up kids from daycare. It's the casual conversations over drinks where important decisions are made—conversations that happen when you're already on your way home.

It's the unspoken expectation that you'll work like you don't have children and raise children like you don't have a demanding career. It's the constant guilt, the feeling that you're never doing enough in either sphere, that you're always letting someone down.

The system perpetuates this penalty through a thousand small decisions, each one seemingly reasonable in isolation. "Let's give this project to someone without family obligations." "She probably doesn't want the travel required for this role." "We need someone who can be fully flexible with their time."

The slow lane becomes crowded with talented women who were never given a real chance to prove themselves under the new constraints of motherhood. Their skills didn't diminish when they became mothers—in many cases, they became sharper, more focused, more efficient. But the perception of their value changed, and in the corporate world, perception often matters more than reality.

The Broader Implications

What troubles me most is how this penalty affects not just individual women, but entire organizations and society as a whole. When we systematically sideline mothers, we lose their perspectives, their enhanced efficiency, their ability to multitask and prioritize under pressure. We lose the innovations that come from people who understand complexity and competing demands.

Companies talk endlessly about wanting diverse perspectives and inclusive cultures, but then they create systems that push out half the population as soon as they start families. They wonder why they struggle with retention of high-performing women, why their leadership teams lack diversity, why their culture feels stagnant.

The answer is often right in front of them: they've created an environment where having children is effectively a career-limiting move for women, while it enhances men's career prospects (because it demonstrates stability and commitment to providing for a family).

This isn't just a women's issue—it's an economic issue, a competitiveness issue, a fundamental question about what kind of society we want to build. When we make it impossible for talented people to contribute fully because they have families, we all lose.

The motherhood penalty isn't just personal—it's systemic, invisible, and costly for all of us. Every time a talented woman is sidelined, every time a mother's ambition is questioned, we lose more than her potential; we lose the future she could have built. Change won't come from waiting for the "right" time, but from rewriting the rules and demanding better—one courageous decision at a time.

Pearls of Insight

- ❖ **There's Never a Perfect Time:** The "right" time to have children is a myth designed to keep women waiting indefinitely. The world will always find reasons why now isn't ideal. Don't let that stop you from living your life on your own terms.
- ❖ **Support Isn't Always Support:** Sometimes what looks like accommodation or understanding is actually marginalization in disguise. True support means giving women genuine opportunities to excel, not just safe, low-impact work.
- ❖ **The Motherhood Penalty is Systemic:** The perception that mothers are less committed or capable is deeply embedded in organizational cultures. It takes conscious, sustained effort to challenge and change these assumptions.

- ❖ **Women Can Be Gatekeepers Too:** Don't assume that women will automatically support other women. Sometimes those who haven't walked your path can be the least sympathetic to your struggles.
- ❖ **Boundaries Are Strategic, Not Selfish:** Setting clear, non-negotiable boundaries isn't just about work-life balance—it's about sustainable high performance. When you respect your own time and energy, others learn to respect it too.
- ❖ **Visibility and Strategy Matter More Than Ever:** After becoming a mother, you can't afford to coast or accept mediocre assignments. Strategic project choices and personal brand management become critical for long-term career success.
- ❖ **Efficiency Increases Under Constraint:** The productivity paradox of motherhood is real. Limited time often leads to enhanced focus, better prioritization, and more meaningful output.

Your Turn: Reflect and Explore

Take time to examine your own experiences or observations about motherhood and career. Use these prompts for reflection or journaling:

1. **Have you experienced or witnessed the motherhood penalty in action?** What specific behaviours or decisions revealed underlying biases about working mothers?
2. **Who are the gatekeepers in your professional environment?** How do they influence opportunities for parents, and how might their own experiences shape their attitudes?
3. **What boundaries do you need to establish to protect your effectiveness and well-being?** How can you communicate these boundaries with confidence rather than apology?

4. **How can you support colleagues who are navigating work and family demands?** What would genuine support look like, beyond surface-level accommodation?
5. **If you're a parent, what changes would make you feel truly valued and supported at work?** If you're not a parent, how can you advocate for policies and practices that support working families?
6. **What assumptions about working mothers exist in your organization or industry?** How might these assumptions be limiting talent and reducing organizational effectiveness?
7. **What's one specific action you can take to challenge the motherhood penalty in your environment?** How can you help create a culture where having children enhances rather than limits career prospects?

As I learned to navigate these impossible choices, I realized that true progress isn't about perfect timing—it's about refusing to let anyone else define your limits. The next chapter is about what happens when you claim your space anyway, and lead on your own terms.

CHAPTER 21
Systemic Barriers – When Systems Keep People Out

We're told that hard work and merit will open every door—but what if the system itself is the lock? My fifth rejection from a mining company wasn't just disappointing; it was a wake-up call. I realized I wasn't up against a lack of skill or effort, but an invisible wall built into the very process meant to be fair.

The Mining Company and the Invisible Wall

Years ago, I set my sights on a role at a major mining company. It was the kind of company that boasted about its values—fairness, diversity, meritocracy. I was excited. I believed I had the skills and experience they needed. I applied not once, but five times, each time for a different role. Each time, I was met with the same result: rejection.

The application process was a labyrinth. It started with an online form, then a series of automated assessments, followed by personality quizzes, and finally, a video interview platform that used algorithm to analyze your responses. Each rejection came swiftly, with a polite, generic email: "Thank you for your interest. Unfortunately, you have not been selected to progress further." There was no feedback, no explanation, just a sense that I had been filtered out by a process that didn't even allow a human to see my application.

At first, I blamed myself. Maybe my resume wasn't strong enough. Maybe I didn't answer the questions in the right way. But after the fifth rejection, I started to wonder: was it really me, or was it the system?

The Executive Leader Story

A few years later, fate brought me back to that same mining company, but this time as a consultant. I was hired to help with a diversity and inclusion initiative. One afternoon, over coffee, I shared my experience with the Executive Leader I was working with. He listened intently, then surprised me with his own story.

"You know," he said, "when I first tried to get a job here, I applied twenty times. I kept getting rejected. Then, out of frustration, I changed my name on the application to something more Western-sounding. Suddenly, I got through to the next stage."

He shook his head, still bewildered. "They always say it's the process, the system, that's filtering candidates. But the only thing I changed was my name. Everything else was the same."

His story floored me. Here was a senior leader, someone who had made it to the top, admitting that even he had to game the system to get a foot in the door. If this was his experience, what hope did others have?

The Algorithmic Gatekeeper

The company prided itself on its "objective" recruitment process. They had invested heavily in technology—automated screening tools, algorithm-driven assessments, and data analytics—to remove human bias. But as the executive leaders story revealed, these systems were far from neutral. They had simply automated the bias, making it faster and harder to detect.

When I dug deeper, I found that the algorithms were trained on historical hiring data. If, in the past, the company had favoured candidates with certain names, backgrounds, or qualifications, the algorithm learned to do the same. The result? Qualified candidates were being filtered out before a human ever saw their application.

This is what we call a **systemic barrier**—a hidden obstacle built into the very processes that are supposed to ensure fairness. It's not always intentional. In fact, it's often the result of good intentions gone awry. But the impact is real, and it's devastating.

The Indigenous Quota Dilemma

My work with the company didn't stop at recruitment. I was also involved in Indigenous engagement projects. The executive leaders often lamented their struggle to meet diversity quotas. "We want to hire Indigenous people," he'd say, "but we're just not getting any applicants through the process."

I decided to investigate. I looked at their recruitment pipeline, from the initial application to the final offer. What I found was a maze of barriers—each one seemingly small, but together forming an almost impenetrable wall.

First, there was the online application, which required a stable internet connection and a computer—something not always available in remote Indigenous communities. Then there were lengthy assessments, many of which were culturally biased or irrelevant to the roles being filled. Finally, there were strict selection criteria: university degrees, high grades, specific technical qualifications.

The company wanted "the best of the best," but the reality was that many Indigenous candidates hadn't had the same educational opportunities. Most had completed TAFE (Technical and Further Education) courses, which are highly practical and respected, but not always recognized by the company's automated systems.

The Selection Criteria Trap

We brought this up with the leadership team. "You've set the bar so high," I said, "that you're automatically excluding the very people you want to hire. This isn't about merit—it's about access."

Together, we reviewed the roles. We identified twelve positions where a TAFE qualification was more than sufficient. These were jobs where practical skills mattered more than academic credentials. We proposed a new pathway: hire candidates with TAFE qualifications, give them on-the-job training, and support them to pursue further education while working.

It wasn't easy. Changing the criteria required sign-off from multiple departments—HR, legal, operations, and the executive team. There was resistance. "We have to maintain our standards," some argued. "We can't lower the bar."

But the quota was a hard target. The company's reputation—and, frankly, some bonuses—depended on meeting it. Eventually, the rules were bent, processes were streamlined, and the new pathway was approved.

The result? A wave of talented, motivated Indigenous employees who brought fresh perspectives and skills to the company. But it shouldn't have taken a crisis to make this change. The system had been broken all along—it just took a quota and a lot of advocacy to fix it.

The AI Recruitment Scandal

This isn't just a local problem. Around the world, companies are turning to AI to streamline recruitment. The promise is objectivity, speed, and efficiency. But the reality is often very different.

Take the case of a major American tech company. They implemented an AI-driven recruitment tool to screen applicants. The AI was trained on ten years of hiring data. Historically, the company had hired eight men for every two women. The AI learned this pattern and replicated it, systematically favouring male candidates and filtering out women.

When the bias was discovered, the company tried to blame the AI. But the truth was clear: the AI had simply learned from the company's own practices. The systemic barrier wasn't the technology—it was the data, the process, the culture.

It was a wake-up call, not just for them, but for the entire industry. AI doesn't remove bias. It amplifies it—unless we're vigilant about what we're teaching it.

Passive-Aggressive Compliance

I see this pattern everywhere I go. I work with HR teams on diversity, equity, and inclusion (DEI) initiatives. In workshops, people nod along, say all the right things, and express support for DEI. But when it comes to changing processes, the resistance is palpable.

"I really support DEI," they say, "but it's so unfortunate—these candidates just didn't meet our criteria. They couldn't get through the process."

This is passive-aggressive compliance. On the surface, it looks like support. But underneath, it's a refusal to change. The criteria remain the same. The processes remain the same. And the outcomes remain the same.

We run workshops, share lived experiences, and challenge teams to rethink their systems. Sometimes, we make progress. But often, when proposals go up the chain, they're met with a blanket statement: "Keep things simple. Have an equitable process. Same process for everyone."

A few months later, the same leaders lament that they're not meeting their targets. They implement quick fixes—tactical moves to hit quotas, because their bonuses depend on it. But these aren't strategic, long-term solutions. They're band-aids on a broken system.

The Illusion of Fairness

The most insidious thing about systemic barriers is that they're often invisible to those who benefit from them. "Same process for everyone" sounds fair. But it ignores the reality that not everyone starts from the same place.

Imagine a race where some runners start at the starting line, while others start a hundred meters behind. If you judge everyone by who crosses the finish line first, you're not measuring talent—you're measuring privilege.

That's what systemic barriers do. They bake inequality into the process, then call the outcome "merit."

The Human Cost

Behind every statistic, every failed application, every unmet quota, there's a real person. Someone who had the skills, the passion, the drive—but was filtered out by a process that never saw them.

I think about the Indigenous candidates who never made it past the first screen. The women who were filtered out by AI. The applicants with "foreign" names who never got a callback. The single mothers who couldn't attend late-night interviews because they had no childcare. The people with disabilities who were excluded by inaccessible online forms.

These aren't isolated incidents. They're the predictable result of systems designed without equity in mind.

The Role of Leadership

Changing these systems isn't easy. It takes courage, persistence, and a willingness to challenge the status quo. It requires leaders who are willing to listen, to learn, and to act.

I've seen what happens when leaders take this seriously. Processes are redesigned. Criteria are re-evaluated. Barriers are identified and removed. The result is a more diverse, more inclusive, and ultimately more successful organization.

But I've also seen what happens when leaders pay lip service to change. The barriers remain. The outcomes don't improve. And the organization misses out on the talent and perspectives it desperately needs.

The Power of Data—and Its Limits

Data can be a powerful tool for identifying and addressing systemic barriers. But it's not enough to collect data—we have to ask the right questions.

- ❖ Who is applying, and who is getting through each stage of the process?
- ❖ Where are candidates dropping out, and why?
- ❖ What patterns emerge when we break down the data by gender, ethnicity, disability, or other factors?

Too often, organizations stop at surface-level metrics. They track the number of applicants, the number of hires, the percentage of women or minorities in the workforce. But they don't dig deeper to understand the barriers in the process.

Data can tell us where the problems are. But it takes human insight—and the will to act—to fix them.

The Myth of the Neutral System

One of the biggest myths in business is the idea of the "neutral" system. The belief that if we remove human judgment, we remove bias. But every system is designed by people. Every algorithm is trained on human data. Every process reflects the values and assumptions of its creators.

Neutrality is an illusion. The question isn't whether our systems have bias—it's what kind of bias they have, and what we're doing about it.

The Way Forward

So what can we do? How do we dismantle systemic barriers and build processes that are truly fair and inclusive?

It starts with awareness. We have to be willing to see the barriers, even when they're invisible to us. We have to listen to the experiences of those who are excluded, and believe them.

Next, we have to examine our systems—every form, every algorithm, every criterion. We have to ask: Who does this help? Who does it hurt? Who gets left out?

We need to be willing to change. That means rethinking our criteria, redesigning our processes, and holding ourselves accountable for outcomes—not just intentions.

It means using data wisely, but never letting it replace human judgment. It means investing in training, mentorship, and support for those who have been excluded.

And most of all, it means leadership. Leaders set the tone. They decide whether diversity and inclusion are priorities or just buzzwords. They have the power to change the system—or to keep it exactly as it is.

Systemic barriers aren't just policies or algorithms—they're stories we tell ourselves about fairness while quietly locking out those who don't fit the mold. True change begins when we stop mistaking process for progress and start dismantling the walls we've built in the name of neutrality.

Pearls of Insight

- ❖ **Systemic barriers are often invisible but deeply entrenched.** They're built into processes, criteria, and algorithms that seem neutral but have unequal impacts.
- ❖ **"Same process for everyone" isn't always fair.** True equity recognizes that people start from different places and need different kinds of support.
- ❖ **AI can amplify human bias if we're not careful.** Technology is not a solution unless we're vigilant about what we're teaching it.
- ❖ **Good intentions are not enough.** The impact of our systems matters more than our intentions.
- ❖ **Passive-aggressive compliance keeps barriers in place.** Real change requires more than ticking boxes and meeting quotas.
- ❖ **Data is a tool, not a solution.** Use it to identify barriers, but don't let it replace human insight and accountability.
- ❖ **Leadership is key.** Leaders have the power to change systems—but only if they're willing to listen, learn, and act.

Your Turn: Reflect and Explore

Pause and examine the systems and processes around you. Use these prompts to guide your reflection or journaling:

1. **Where do you see systemic barriers in your workplace or community?** What processes or criteria might be excluding people without you realizing it?

2. **Have you ever been filtered out by a system?** How did it feel? What did you learn from the experience?
3. **What assumptions underlie your organization's recruitment or promotion processes?** Are they truly necessary, or just tradition?
4. **How is technology being used in your organization?** Is it making things fairer, or just automating old biases?
5. **What would it look like to design a truly equitable process?** Who would you involve? What changes would you make?
6. **How can you use your position—no matter how small—to advocate for change?** Who are your allies? What data or stories can you share?
7. **If you're a leader, how are you holding yourself and your team accountable for outcomes, not just intentions?** What are you willing to change?

As I confronted the reality of these invisible barriers, I knew the next challenge would be even harder: moving from awareness to action, and finding the courage to lead change in systems that resist it at every turn.

CHAPTER 22
Women and Ambition

What if ambition in women wasn't a problem to be managed, but a power the world desperately needs? From playground negotiations to boardroom battles, I learned early that the same drive celebrated in men is seen as a threat in women. My story is just one among thousands—each one proof that the mountain of bias isn't moving on its own.

We have this stereotypical notion about ambition. It's liked, admired, and respected in a man. In a woman, it's frowned upon, looked at negatively, even feared. There are loads of books, podcasts, and research studies dedicated to this phenomenon. Yet nobody has solved it. We speak about it, we listen to the findings, we nod our heads knowingly, and then we move on. My story is just another addition to the overflowing mountain of evidence that this problem clearly exists. But it's a mountain that refuses to move.

The irony is that I was raised to be ambitious. My father encouraged us to study, to dream big, to reach for more. When my older sister and I were little, we'd spend weekends and holidays at the construction site yard where he ran his business. It was our playground, our second home, our unofficial business school.

Early Lessons in Leadership

When Dad left for meetings, my sister would march into his office, settle into his big leather chair, and call me in as her secretary to take notes. I can still picture her, all of eight years old, sitting behind that enormous desk, trying to look serious and important. I'd get upset and demand my turn to be the boss. She rarely gave in—older sister privileges, I suppose. But I learned to be strategic. I'd make sure she didn't come to the yard on certain days, and then it was my turn to play CEO.

As girls, we were role-playing being the boss, being the leader. Nobody stopped us. Nobody told us we were being inappropriate or too ambitious. We'd listen in on contractual discussions and negotiations at the office, and hear my parents discuss it at home over dinner. We didn't realize it then, but we were being trained. I fell in love with business, finance, and mathematics. The language of deals and strategy became as familiar to me as bedtime stories.

There was the usual imbalance—my brother was still the golden boy in our Indian family—but I was rebellious. I challenged it at every opportunity. I was extremely sporty and competitive. Because we weren't well off, I realized a trick: while other kids were complacent and comfortable, I sharpened my talents to win competitions and prizes. Money was tight, but trophies were free if you could earn them.

I became so good at this that one charity organization had to stop me from entering their competitions because they knew I had a serious chance of winning every time. They needed to give other kids a chance.

So yes, I was ambitious. Competitive. When I started work, I was collaborative, but I was also strategic. I wanted more. I wanted to excel, to lead, to make a difference. I think that drive sits at the core of who I am. It's tied to my desire for excellence—for myself, my clients, my community.

The First Reality Check

But slowly, I started to notice something. I interviewed for a job in Kenya very early in my career. The CEO, an old Indian man, looked at me across his desk and asked, "Why should we invest in you? You'll get married, have kids, and give up work. We'd be wasting our time hiring you."

The words hit like a slap. Not only was he questioning my commitment, but he was also offering to pay me peanuts, provide no training, and expect me to work my butt off. The message was clear: your ambition doesn't matter because you're a woman, and women are temporary employees.

But I fought back. I told him I would prioritize my career. I spoke with conviction about my goals and my dedication. Eventually, I made the decision to move back to London, where I hoped my ambitions would be taken more seriously.

Learning the Game

In London, I worked at a job, early in my career, where I poured everything into my role. I exceeded expectations, delivered results, and went above and beyond. At the end of the year review, they told me it wasn't enough. My bonus was £500—not even enough to cover a decent vacation. No promotion, no pay increase. I had exceeded expectations, and this was my reward.

I refused to accept it. I proactively reached out and changed teams, finding a place where my talent was recognized, respected, and valued. I made a rule for myself: I would not stay in jobs or positions where I wasn't respected. Life's too short to dim your light for people who can't see it.

Companies generally didn't invest in training—even now, I hear about the minimal budgets they allocate for employee development. But living in London, I realized there were tons of one- or two-day conferences, often free, featuring powerful speakers like Tony Robbins and other thought leaders. I'd go on my own time, at my own cost, and get upskilled. If they wouldn't invest in me, I'd invest in myself.

The Contractor Strategy

I also became a contractor. I noticed that as a permanent employee, they'd throw work at you, drown you in busy work, and then someone who was doing okay but networking well would get promoted. As a contractor, I had a rule: only one project at a time, and I'd make it a bloody success.

From the sidelines, I watched permanent employees get burned out, working insane hours, sacrificing their kids' school performances and dates with their partners, all in the hope that if they did more, they'd get recognized and rewarded. So many of them ended up on stress leave or getting fired. The system was broken, but they kept feeding into it.

When I came to Australia, I went permanent again. In one of those roles, I delivered a remarkable organizational transformation—new ways of working, agile methodologies, customer centricity, cultural change. It was transformative work. I had seven nominations for an industry award. The impact was undeniable.

The C-Suite Betrayal

I wanted a C-suite position. I had mapped out everything—the relationships, the deliverables, the value I'd created. I had made these leaders look good, done the groundwork, proven my capabilities. But I didn't know the unspoken rules of the C-suite game.

I asked one C-suite leader to be my sponsor, mentor, and advocate. I wanted him to get me a seat at the table and teach me the ropes. On one of our walks, he looked at me seriously and said, "You're too ambitious." He said it like it was a character flaw. "You're too driven, you move too fast. If I'm going to do this for you, I need you to promise me four years of service and to tame down your ambition and pace."

I was desperate. I agreed.

I crafted a role for myself: Chief Customer Experience Officer. We defined it, socialized it, built support for it. Then one day, a senior male leader—a great guy who'd been there a long time—resigned. They wanted to keep him.

And bang—just like that, they gave him my well-crafted role. They told me some bullshit story and tried to offer me a mediocre "Head of Something" position instead.

Just like that. My ambition, my planning, my carefully crafted role—handed to someone else because they were afraid of losing him.

The Pattern Emerges

Each one of these experiences was challenging. They crushed my spirit, sapped my confidence, stole my mojo. But every time I hit rock bottom, I chose to choose myself. Even with shattered confidence, I'd advocate for myself and go out to find something right for me.

This became a pattern I started to recognize everywhere. Women's ambition was treated like a problem to be managed rather than a strength to be leveraged. We were told to "tone it down," "be more collaborative," "wait your turn." Men with the same drive were called "visionary" and "leadership material."

I watched ambitious women get labeled as "difficult," "pushy," or "not a team player." I saw them passed over for promotions because they were "too aggressive" or because leadership was "concerned about their work-life balance"—code for "she has kids" or "she might have kids."

The double bind was impossible. Be ambitious, and you're too much. Be collaborative, and you lack leadership presence. Speak up, and you're aggressive. Stay quiet, and you're not executive material.

The Self-Advocacy Awakening

But here's what I learned: self-advocacy is a powerful strength. You find it at the bottom of the barrel of broken confidence, hope, and despair. When you're stripped of everything else—the support you thought you had, the promises that were broken, the recognition you earned but never received—that's when you discover you have a choice.

You can accept the crumbs, or you can choose yourself.

I chose myself. Not because I was fearless—I was terrified. Not because I was confident—my confidence was in pieces. But because I realized that no one else was going to advocate for me the way I could advocate for myself.

Self-advocacy isn't about being selfish or difficult. It's about recognizing your worth and refusing to settle for less. It's about understanding that your ambition is not a character flaw—it's a superpower that the world desperately needs.

The Cost of Conformity

I think about all the ambitious women who did tame themselves down, who did promise four years of service in exchange for the possibility of recognition. What happened to their dreams? What innovations were lost because they dimmed their light? What problems remained unsolved because they chose conformity over courage?

The world tells women that our ambition makes others uncomfortable, so we should make ourselves smaller. But the world needs our ambition. It needs our drive, our vision, our refusal to accept the status quo. Every time we diminish ourselves to make others comfortable, we rob the world of what we could have contributed.

The Ambition Advantage

Here's the truth they don't tell you: ambition in women is not just acceptable—it's essential. We bring different perspectives, different approaches, different solutions. Our ambition is informed by our lived experiences of having to work twice as hard for half the recognition. It's tempered by our understanding of what it means to be overlooked and underestimated.

When ambitious women lead, they remember what it felt like to be on the outside. They create opportunities for others. They build inclusive cultures. They solve problems that others didn't even know existed.

But first, we have to embrace our ambition. We have to stop apologizing for wanting more, for dreaming bigger, for refusing to settle. We have to stop asking for permission to be excellent.

Breaking the Pattern

The mountain of evidence isn't going to move itself. Change happens when ambitious women refuse to be tamed, when we choose ourselves even when others won't choose us, when we create our own opportunities instead of waiting for them to be given.

It happens when we support other ambitious women instead of seeing them as competition. When we mentor the next generation and teach them that their ambition is not a problem to be solved but a gift to be shared.

It happens when we stop asking for a seat at the table and start building our own tables—bigger, more inclusive tables where ambition is celebrated regardless of gender.

The Strength in the Struggle

Every rejection, every broken promise, every time someone tried to dim my light—it all led me to the same place: the understanding that my worth isn't determined by others' recognition of it. My ambition isn't a character flaw that needs fixing. It's the engine that drives me to create, to lead, to make a difference.

The struggle taught me self-reliance. The disappointments taught me resilience. The betrayals taught me discernment. And the moments when I chose myself despite it all—those taught me that I am enough, exactly as I am.

Every time I chose myself, even when my confidence was shattered, I reclaimed a piece of my power. Ambition isn't a flaw to be fixed—it's the engine that drives change, creates opportunity, and lights the way for others. The world will keep trying to tame ambitious women, but the future belongs to those who refuse to shrink.

Pearls of Insight

- **Ambition in women is not a character flaw—it's a superpower.** The world needs women who refuse to settle, who dream big, and who push boundaries.
- **Self-advocacy is found in the depths of disappointment.** When everything else fails, the choice to champion yourself becomes your greatest strength.
- **The double bind is real, but you don't have to play by its rules.** Create your own path instead of trying to fit into someone else's narrow definition of acceptable behaviour.
- **Your worth isn't determined by others' recognition of it.** External validation is nice, but internal conviction is necessary.
- **Every "no" is information, not a verdict.** Use rejection as data to refine your approach, not as evidence that you should give up.

❖ **Supporting other ambitious women breaks the cycle.** When we lift each other up, we change the entire landscape for the next generation.

Your Turn: Reflect and Explore

Take a moment to examine your relationship with ambition. Use these prompts to guide your reflection:

1. **How do you define ambition for yourself?** What does it look like when you're operating at your highest potential?
2. **When have you been told to "tone it down" or "be more collaborative"?** How did that feedback affect your behaviour and your confidence?
3. **What dreams have you shelved because they seemed "too ambitious"?** What would it look like to dust them off and pursue them now?
4. **Who are the ambitious women in your life who inspire you?** How can you learn from their examples and support their continued success?
5. **Where do you need to practice better self-advocacy?** What opportunities or recognition are you waiting for instead of actively pursuing?
6. **How can you use your ambition to create opportunities for others?** What doors can you open for the next generation of ambitious women?
7. **What would you attempt if you knew that your ambition was welcomed and celebrated?**

As I embraced ambition as my superpower, the next challenge became clear: how do we create spaces where every woman's drive is not just accepted, but celebrated—and how do we lift as we climb, so no one is left behind?

CHAPTER 23

The Unseen Current — Purpose, Privilege, and Paying It Forward

What if the real force shaping your life isn't talent or ambition, but invisible currents—history, privilege, and the doors opened or slammed shut before you ever arrived? My story, like so many others, has been shaped as much by the margins as by the moments in the spotlight. Purpose, I've learned, isn't born in a vacuum; it's forged in the tension between what we inherit and what we choose to do with it.

What Shapes Us: History, Marginalization, and the Seeds of Purpose

Every career, every life, is shaped by currents you can't always see. Some are legacies of privilege or deprivation, some are inherited stories, some are the result of doors opened (or slammed shut) because of who you are, where you're from, or how you're perceived. Purpose is rarely born in a vacuum — it's shaped by personal history, by the experience of marginalization or access, by being the outsider or the insider, by learning who has power and who doesn't, and what you choose to do with what you're given.

For me, purpose has always felt like an undercurrent. It's not just about what I want to build or achieve for myself — it's about what I can give, how I can use the platforms I've fought for (and sometimes been handed) to open doors and lift up others. In the boardroom, in community, in family, I've learned that stewardship — not ownership — is the only lasting legacy. If I have privilege, it's not for hoarding. It's for paying it forward.

This is the story of learning that lesson, sometimes the hard way. It's about how ego and legacy, pride and purpose, collide and co-exist. And it's about how navigating those tensions, in work and in life, shapes the kind of leader — and human — I want to be.

The Boardroom: Mirror, Battleground, and Classroom

When I stepped into my first serious board role, I felt like I'd finally made it. As a woman of colour, moving into rooms that, for generations, had been closed to people who looked like me, I carried a private sense of victory. But right behind it came an almost physical anxiety: Would I belong? Would I be taken seriously? Was I ready for the responsibility?

I wanted to make a difference, to be the catalyst for transformation. But I knew enough to start by learning the lay of the land: the unspoken rules, the power structures, the stubborn roots of tradition. It's one thing to have a vision for change; it's another to understand whether the organization is ready for it.

In those early days, nerves surfaced in my voice — too fast, too eager, afraid of missing my shot to prove I deserved my seat. I threw myself into committee work, trying to make an impact through action. When I later became Chair of the Game Changer Awards, I felt the power (and responsibility) of being able to articulate a vision. But with every win, I could feel the tendrils of personal attachment wrapping around the role. It's incredibly seductive — that feeling of being needed, being at the center, being the one who makes things happen.

As more opportunities came my way, I adopted a mantra: **Check your ego at the door.** Every meeting, every event, was a chance to practice humility — to focus on purpose, not position. I gravitated towards leaders who were authentic, who led by listening, who understood that leadership is about stewardship, not self-promotion.

But even with the best intentions, the work was never frictionless.

Resistance, Renewal, and the Realities of Change

Progress, especially in organizations built on tradition, is tough. Sometimes, it means parting ways with people who've been there longest. Not because they're bad, but because their mindset or working style doesn't fit the new direction — a direction grounded in collaboration, diversity, equity, and inclusion.

Those were some of the hardest moments of my career. For the people leaving, it wasn't just a job or a volunteer role — it was a piece of their identity. Cutting ties felt brutal, like an amputation. It was personal, not just organizational. Old grievances, entrenched habits, and past politics bubbled up, clouding the real goal: serving the mission.

Letting people go was painful, but clearing space for new energy, new ideas, and broader inclusion was transformative. The organization found a refreshed sense of purpose, and the wider community responded with enthusiasm. That's the paradox of stewardship: the most meaningful change often requires letting go — of people, of practices, of your own sense of control.

The Family Mirror: Seeing My Father's Struggle

Strangely enough, I'd seen this play out before — not in a boardroom, but in my own family. My father was a pillar of our community, the founding chairman of our community temple in Nakuru. He poured decades of sacrifice, time, and money into building not just a place of worship, but a center of belonging. His identity was inseparable from his role. He was "the leader." Respected, influential, indispensable.

Then, the inevitable: the next generation wanted their turn. The high priest, who'd once handpicked my father, decided he was done and replaced him with someone younger. My father was devastated. It wasn't just losing a title — it was losing a core part of himself. Power, influence, respect, even his sense of worth, seemed to vanish overnight.

The story didn't end there. In a move that only made things messier, the high priest kept my dad around as Vice Chair, hoping to maintain continuity (and, let's be honest, donations). The result? Intergenerational warfare. The younger leaders wanted to innovate. My dad, feeling threatened, clung harder to his old ways. The high priest played puppet-master, trying to balance the old guard and the new.

Watching my father's heartbreak — and his slow process of letting go — taught me more about stewardship than any formal leadership training. I saw, up close, how easy it is to let a role become your identity, how hard it is to step aside gracefully, and how necessary it is for organizations (and people) to evolve.

Privilege, Marginalization, and the Double Edge of Belonging

Privilege is a word that gets thrown around a lot, often as an accusation or a source of guilt. But real privilege is complicated. I've been both outsider and insider, marginalized and included, sometimes in the same room. I've felt what it's like to be underestimated, to have to work twice as hard for half the recognition. But I've also, over time, accumulated advantages: education, access, reputation, networks.

The question is not whether you have privilege, but what you do with it. Do you cling to it, use it to block others out, or do you pay it forward? Do you use your voice to amplify those who've been silenced? Do you open doors behind you, or close them?

Purpose, for me, is about stewardship of whatever privilege I have. It's about remembering where I started, who helped me, and how I can create space for others. It's about understanding that "making it" isn't the finish line — it's the starting point for lifting up the next person in line.

Ego, Legacy, and the Dance of Detachment

Here's the hardest lesson: the more you care, the easier it is to confuse your role with your identity. The more you achieve, the more tempting it is to believe you're indispensable. But true stewardship is about making yourself unnecessary. It's about building systems, cultures, and pipelines so strong that they thrive after you're gone.

Whenever I feel my ego flaring up — that urge to be the hero, to get the credit, to be "the one" — I remind myself: **The job is temporary. The mission is permanent.** My job is to serve, not to own. My legacy is the doors I help open, not the spotlight I occupy.

And when it's time to move on, the healthiest thing I can do is let go with grace. To be passionate about the purpose, but detached about the position. That's how you make room for new leaders, new ideas, and new energy.

The Invisible Threads: Margins, Memory, and Meaning

It's easy to think of leadership as a solo act, but every boardroom, every team, every family is shaped by invisible threads: who gets a seat at the table, whose stories get told, who's encouraged to speak, who's asked to wait. My own path has been shaped as much by the doors that were closed as the ones that opened.

- ❖ The teacher who believed in me when nobody else did.
- ❖ The boss who gave me a shot, even when I wasn't the obvious candidate.
- ❖ The family members who made sacrifices I'll never fully understand.

I owe my place, in part, to the privileges I inherited and the mentors who paid it forward. That's why stewardship — not just achievement — matters so much to me. I'm not just building for myself. I'm building for the people who come after, for the ones who might never know my name but will benefit from the work.

The Stewardship Mindset in Action Boardrooms and Beyond

Stewardship means seeing every leadership role as a trust, not a trophy. It's about asking, every day: Am I serving the organization's purpose, or just protecting my own legacy? Am I making decisions that will stand the test of time, or just the test of my own tenure?

- ❖ **Identity vs. Role:** When I sense my self-worth getting tangled up with my title, I pause. I remind myself that I'm more than this position — and so is everyone else.

Over-identification breeds fear, resistance to change, and, ultimately, irrelevance.
- ❖ **Succession as Evolution:** I now see succession not as a threat, but as the ultimate act of leadership. Preparing others, welcoming fresh ideas, stepping aside with dignity — this is how organizations stay alive, and leaders stay relevant.
- ❖ **Detachment Enables Grace:** Healthy detachment doesn't mean apathy. It means loving the mission more than the role. It means letting go, even (especially) when it's hard, because you care about the people and the purpose more than your own sense of control.
- ❖ **Impact Over Permanence:** Focus on what you can give, not what you can keep. The most powerful legacies are often the ones that outlast your name on the door.

Lessons from Both Sides of the Transition

I've seen leadership transitions that were graceful — and some that were agonizing. The difference almost always comes down to ego. The leaders who clung the hardest, who made their roles their whole identity, left behind chaos and resentment. The ones who let go with generosity, who celebrated their successors, built something that lasted.

The lesson? Prepare to leave before you have to. Mentor the next generation. Share knowledge freely. Celebrate progress, even when you're not at the center of it.

Privilege is never just a possession—it's a responsibility. The most lasting legacy isn't what you build for yourself, but the doors you open for others. Every day, I ask myself: How can I use what I've been given to make it easier for someone else? That's the unseen current. That's the legacy worth leaving.

Pearls of Insight

- ❖ **Purpose is shaped by history and privilege.** You don't choose the currents that shape you, but you do choose how to respond. Your story — and the ways you've been helped or hindered — fuel your purpose.
- ❖ **Stewardship is about paying it forward.** The real test of leadership is what you leave behind: not just what you built, but the opportunities you created for others.

Reflect & Explore

1. **How has your history shaped your purpose?** What are the moments of pain, triumph, exclusion, or belonging that fuel your drive? What have you inherited — good and bad — from your family, culture, community? How does that shape the way you lead and serve?
2. **How can you use your privilege to lift others?** Where do you have a voice, a seat at the table, an opportunity others don't? How can you use those advantages to open doors, amplify voices, and build pathways for those still on the margins?

As I continue to navigate these currents, the next chapter calls for action: transforming awareness into impact, and finding new ways to pay it forward—so the story doesn't end with me, but begins anew for those still waiting at the margins.

PART V
BUILDING A LEGACY OF IMPACT & INCLUSION

CHAPTER 24
Becoming the Beacon

What if the role model you've been searching for never arrives—and you're called to become that beacon yourself? In the crowded corridors of London's investment banks, I kept looking for someone who looked like me, someone who had blazed a trail I could follow. But the faces at the top were distant, and sometimes, the few women who made it seemed determined to pull the ladder up behind them. That's when I made a promise: If I ever broke through, I'd make sure the path was wider and brighter for those coming after me.

From Seeking Role Models to Becoming One

For much of my early career, I was always looking up — searching for someone a little further along the path, someone who looked like me and had managed to break through. In the sharp corners and high rises of London's investment banks, especially in the world of technology and innovation, that search often felt like a losing game. The halls were crowded, but I rarely saw a face or heard a voice that told me I belonged, or that my story could ever land at the center of this industry.

The few women who did make it to the top seemed either impossibly distant or, more confusingly, sometimes even tougher on those coming up behind them. I remember one senior woman — sharp suit, sharper tongue — who seemed to take a certain satisfaction in making things a little harder for the next wave. Maybe she thought it built character, maybe she'd internalized the culture, or maybe she was just tired of always being "the only one." I couldn't know, but I felt the sting all the same.

It was then that I made myself a promise, almost defiantly: if I ever reached a position of influence, I'd work to be the kind of role model I'd always needed. Not just a name on a list, not just a seat at the table, but a beacon. Someone visible, accessible, and determined to make the path wider and smoother for others.

Representation Matters

It's hard to overstate the power of seeing yourself in someone else's success. The old phrase — "you have to see her to be her" — rings true. For those of us who spent years feeling like outliers, seeing someone with your background, your accent, your skin tone, or your story not just survive but thrive, rewires what you believe is possible.

Representation isn't just symbolic. It's practical. When people from marginalized or underrepresented groups step into leadership roles, it changes the questions that get asked, the problems that get solved, and the doors that get opened. It changes who gets mentored, who gets sponsored, who gets believed in.

But representation also comes with responsibility. The higher you climb, the more you realize that someone is always watching, always wondering if it can be done. You become a living answer to the question: "Is there a place for someone like me here?"

Be the Beacon You Once Needed

That promise to "be the change" became my north star. I carried it with me through every job, every committee, every yes and every no. But a promise is just a start. The real work is what comes after — the choices you make, and the ways you show up for others.

Mentoring Youth

One of the most rewarding chapters of my life has been mentoring kids from low socio-economic backgrounds, through programs like the Australian Business and Community Network (ABCN). I meet teenagers who have never met anyone who works in banking, tech, or entrepreneurship. Some have never been told, out loud, that they are allowed to dream big. I see myself in them — the uncertainty, the hunger, the tentative ambition.

Mentoring isn't about having all the answers. It's about being a mirror and a megaphone: reflecting back what's possible, and amplifying the belief that they can aim higher. Sometimes all it takes is someone to say, "Yes, you belong here. Yes, you can."

Championing Future Innovators

My work with the Game Changer Awards — first as a judge, now as Chair — has been another way to put this philosophy into action. We bring together kids from Year 3 to Year 12, encouraging not just technical skills but also leadership, collaboration, and self-belief. In 2024, we impacted over 400 kids, many from regional or disadvantaged backgrounds. Our goal is to double that, to reach even more kids who might otherwise never see themselves as "innovators."

I've watched shy, uncertain students transform over the course of the program, stepping up to present their ideas with conviction. Sometimes they need a nudge, sometimes just a smile from someone who understands what it's like to feel out of place. Every time I see a spark ignite — when a kid realizes, "I can solve this, I can lead" — I'm reminded why representation and encouragement matter so much.

Supporting Migrant Women

For fifteen years, in both London and Australia, I've mentored migrant and marginalized women. Many arrive in a new country already accomplished — degrees, careers, whole lives left behind — but suddenly find themselves voiceless, invisible, underestimated. They face prejudice, lose access to networks, and sometimes even question their own worth.

Mentoring here is less about business strategy and more about restoration. It's about helping women rediscover their confidence, find their voice, and build a new sense of community. Sometimes, just knowing that another woman of color made it through is enough to light the way. When I walk into a STEM event or a boardroom and see another woman from a migrant background, I know the difference it makes. It says: you're not alone. You belong.

Driving Diversity from Within

It's not enough to advocate for change from the sidelines; sometimes you have to step into the system to change it. At the 2023 INCITE Awards, I looked around and saw that, out of 35 judges, I was the youngest and the only woman of colour. It would have been easy to be discouraged, but instead I applied for a board position with WAITTA, the organization behind the awards.

Now, I work to bring more diversity to every level: judges, ambassadors, nominees, attendees. I champion the inclusion of people of colour, Indigenous peoples, women, young people, and neurodiverse individuals. Every time a new face joins the table, the conversation changes. The system shifts, bit by bit.

Cultivating Inclusive Teams

During my time leading the enterprise agile transformation at ASX listed Finance Institution, I made it my mission to create real opportunities for women in IT. I coached, advocated, and pushed for fair recognition and pay. Today, this company sends one of the largest contingents of women to the Women in Technology WA conference. We've built a thriving community where women connect, share stories, and lift each other higher.

None of this happened by accident. It took deliberate effort, sometimes uncomfortable conversations, and the willingness to challenge the status quo. But the results — seeing women step into their power, knowing they're supported — are worth every moment.

The Responsibility of Representation

There's a moment, as you become more visible, when you realize you're no longer just representing yourself. Your presence sends a signal. For every young woman, every person of colour, every migrant sitting in the audience, you become a kind of shorthand: proof that it's possible.

This is both a privilege and a burden. Some days, it feels heavy — the weight of expectations, the pressure not to mess up. But most days, it feels like a calling. It pushes me to keep growing, to keep making space, to keep reaching back.

I remember what it felt like to search for role models and come up empty. Now, I try to be the beacon I once needed: visible, accessible, honest about the challenges, and generous with support.

Who Looks Up to You?

One of the most important questions any leader — any person — can ask is: who's watching? Who takes courage from your example? Who feels seen because you showed up?

Sometimes, you won't know the answer. Sometimes, it's a student you met once, a colleague who watched how you handled a tough meeting, a young professional who heard you speak at a conference. The ripple effects are real, even when invisible.

So I try to lead as if someone's always watching — not out of fear, but out of hope. I try to model the values I want to see in the next generation of leaders: kindness, courage, honesty, inclusivity.

How Can You Model the Way?

Role modelling isn't about perfection. It's about visibility, vulnerability, and consistency. It's about letting people see not just the wins, but the doubts and stumbles, too. When I talk to mentees or teams, I'm upfront about the mistakes I've made, the times I've felt like an outsider, the moments I almost gave up.

Being a beacon doesn't mean you have all the answers. It means you're willing to share what you've learned, to encourage others to keep going, and to light the path just a bit more.

You never truly "arrive" as a role model. The journey is ongoing—a cycle of seeking, learning, and giving back. The goal isn't perfection, but presence: showing up, sharing honestly, and leaving the door open a little wider for the next person. Shine brightly. Someone is watching.

Pearls of Insight

- ❖ **Be the Change:** The negative examples you encounter can be just as powerful as the positive ones. Sometimes, witnessing exclusion or cruelty ignites a deeper commitment to lead differently.
- ❖ **Advocacy Requires Action:** Belief is not enough. Real change happens through concrete steps: mentoring, sponsoring, calling out bias, and opening doors.
- ❖ **Representation is Crucial:** Diversity on boards, panels, and leadership teams isn't just optics. It reshapes

priorities, questions, and outcomes. If you want change, step up and be counted.

- ❖ **Champion from Within:** Use whatever influence you have to create opportunities for others. Sometimes the most powerful change comes from steady, quiet advocacy within your own team or organization.
- ❖ **Community Building:** Networks and support groups aren't just nice-to-haves. They're lifelines — places where people find belonging, confidence, and collective power.

Reflect & Explore

1. **Your "Be the Change" Moment:** What experience pushed you to lead differently, to challenge the way things have always been done? Was it seeing injustice, being excluded, or witnessing someone else's courage?
2. **Actionable Advocacy:** What's one thing you could do this month to make a difference? Could you mentor someone, sponsor a project, or speak up in a meeting? Change starts with small acts, repeated often.
3. **Leveraging Your Position:** No matter your title, you have influence. How can you use it to create a more inclusive environment? Is there a policy to challenge, a voice to amplify, a bias to call out?

As I step into the light for others, I realize the real legacy isn't just about breaking barriers—it's about building a community where everyone is empowered to do the same. The next chapter is about how we keep the momentum going, together, so every story has a chance to shine.

CHAPTER 25
Educate a Woman, Uplift Generations

There's a saying that echoes across continents: "Educate a woman, and you educate a generation." But for families like mine, this isn't just a slogan—it's a lived revolution. I come from a line of women for whom school was a distant dream, and from a father whose radical belief in girls' education cracked open a future none of us could have imagined.

I've lived both sides of that story. I come from a line of women for whom education was once a distant dream, and from a father who—despite his own limited schooling—saw beyond the horizon line that hemmed in our village. His belief, almost radical for his time and place, changed not just my life, but the lives of generations to come.

This is the story of what happens when you invest in a girl's mind — and the ripple that never really ends.

The Village That Raised Me — and the Village I Left Behind

My mother-in-law is nearly eighty now. My mother, not far behind. They grew up in rural India, daughters of the farm, in families where children were counted as extra hands before they were seen as minds to be shaped. My mother-in-law had fifteen siblings — fifteen. Some of them were born just to hedge against the hard math of child mortality, or to ensure there'd be someone left to care for parents in old age. Education, if it was discussed at all, was for boys. Girls were expected to work, marry, obey. Their futures were mapped out in the narrow furrows of the farm, their dreams rationed as strictly as food in a lean season.

My father's story started in the same fields, but he carried a different hunger. He went to school only through Year 4 before he, too, was pulled onto the farm. But the taste of learning — and the ache of leaving it behind — never left him. When he married, he made a decision that would change everything: he left his village and set out for Kenya, alone, searching for a future that didn't yet exist.

In the years that followed, he brought his family over. And when it came to his children — daughters included — he refused to let the old rules bind us. He invested in us as students, not just as workers or wives. He faced criticism, even ridicule, from his own sisters and neighbors. Why educate girls? Why spend money on their schooling when they'd just marry and leave? But his logic was simple: if he could build a new life with just a handful of years in school, what could his daughters achieve if given the chance he never had?

That single, stubborn belief — that girls' minds mattered just as much as boys' — was enough to start tipping the scales.

The Ripple of One Decision

Looking back now, I see how much hung on the wire of that choice. My own life has spanned four continents, moved through industries and roles my grandmothers couldn't have imagined, and demanded that I keep learning, unlearning, and relearning as the world changed beneath my feet.

But none of it was inevitable. It all hinged on my father's refusal to let tradition dictate my future. He saw what education could do — not just for a son, but for a daughter. And he had the courage to weather the backlash, to insist that investing in girls was not a waste, but a wager on the future.

Because of him, I grew up knowing that my mind mattered. That I was allowed to dream, and to work for that dream. That the boundaries around me were not walls but starting lines.

A Return to Roots

I went back to my ancestral village recently, years after my family had left. Much of it looked unchanged — the same dusty roads, the same patchwork of fields, the same long afternoons and slow, communal rhythms. But one thing was different, and it shone brighter than anything I remembered: girls were in school. Not just a handful, but whole classrooms of them, crisp uniforms, books in hand, eyes bright with possibility.

They weren't being prepped for lives of service on the farm, or for early marriages. They were being asked about their ambitions. They were being told they could be teachers, doctors, engineers. Their parents — many of whom had grown up like my mother and mother-in-law, with little or no schooling — were encouraging it, sometimes tentatively, sometimes fiercely.

The Math of Multiplication

The truth about educating women is that its impact is never linear. When you educate a girl, you're not just changing her life; you're changing the lives of her family, her children, and her community. Studies show that educated women marry later, have fewer and healthier children, and earn higher incomes. They invest more in their families, prioritize the education of their own kids, and are more likely to become leaders in their communities.

It's a cascade effect: the benefits spill over, generation after generation. What starts as the decision to send one girl to school becomes, over time, a shift in what a whole village dreams for its daughters.

My own family is a living example. My sisters and I, given the chance to learn, have gone on to build careers, raise children who expect to go even further, and serve as advocates and mentors for others. The ripple continues, outward and onward.

Breaking the Cycle

Cycles of poverty, limitation, and silence are stubborn things. They persist not because people don't care, but because the weight of tradition and necessity is hard to shake. In my family, the cycle was work: every child was a worker first, a student if time allowed. My mother-in-law, my mother, their sisters — they did what was expected, and their worlds were small by design.

But all it takes to start breaking the cycle is one person with a different vision. For us, it was my father. For others, it might be a teacher, a mentor, a community leader, or a government policy. The common thread is always the same: someone sees possibility where others see only risk. Someone decides that girls' futures are worth investing in.

Once that decision is made, the cycle begins to shift. It's slow at first, sometimes painful. But it's unstoppable.

Visionary Leadership Breaks Cycles

My father never spoke about "empowerment" or "equity." He didn't have the language of social change. He just knew that education opened doors, and that his daughters deserved those doors as much as his sons. His courage — in the face of skepticism, in the face of tradition, in the face of his own limited schooling — was the catalyst.

This kind of leadership isn't always loud. Sometimes it's quiet and stubborn, a refusal to accept "that's just the way things are." Sometimes it means being shunned or criticized. But it always means holding the line for something better.

When I look at my own life, and at the lives of girls in my ancestral village today, I see what's possible when someone is brave enough to break with the past.

Education as Liberation

For girls in restrictive environments, education is more than a pathway to a better job. It's liberation. It's the ability to make choices — about work, marriage, children, even where to live. It's the difference between a life scripted by others and a life scripted by self.

For my mother and mother-in-law, the lack of education meant limited options. For me and my sisters, education meant the world opened up. It meant that when opportunity knocked, we recognized it. It meant that when we traveled, learned, and grew, we carried our families with us, rewriting the terms of what was possible.

Personal Experience Fuels Advocacy

My father's own lack of schooling made him a fiercer advocate for us. He knew what he'd missed, and he wanted more for his children. I feel the same responsibility now, as a mother and a mentor. Because I know what a difference access to learning made for me, I make it my mission to open those doors for others — especially for girls and women who are still told they can't, or shouldn't, or don't need to.

I mentor, I sponsor, I advocate, and I challenge the quiet biases that still linger in boardrooms and classrooms. Every time I help a young woman see her own potential, I'm paying forward the investment my father made in me.

Migration and Social Change

Moving to Kenya didn't just change my father's fortunes; it changed his worldview. In a new country, far from the constraints of his village, he saw what was possible when tradition loosened its grip. Migration can be a powerful force for transformation — not just economically, but socially. It exposes you to new ideas, new possibilities, and new expectations.

For our family, migration meant access: to schools, to jobs, to a wider world. But it also meant responsibility — the duty to use what we'd gained to help others, back home and in our new communities.

Generational Returns

Investing in women doesn't just add value; it multiplies it. When you educate a woman, you educate her children. You lift her family. You strengthen her community. You change the odds for everyone who comes after.

When I look at my daughters, I see the legacy of a decision made decades ago, in a small village, by a man with little formal learning but immense vision. I see the chain reaction: my sisters and I, our careers, our advocacy, our children's confidence. The ripple keeps going.

The best way to honor those who invested in us is to pay it forward. Every girl educated, every door opened, every stubborn tradition challenged is a ripple that outlasts us all. That's the legacy of my father's belief—and the promise I make to the next generation: to keep opening doors, keep pushing boundaries, and keep believing that when you educate a woman, you uplift the world.

Pearls of Insight

- ❖ **Visionary Leadership Breaks Cycles:** One person's courage to challenge the norm can change everything for those who come next.
- ❖ **Education is Liberation:** For girls, education isn't just about facts and figures — it's about freedom, agency, and choice.
- ❖ **Personal Experience Fuels Advocacy:** When you know what's at stake, you fight harder to open doors for others.
- ❖ **Migration Can Drive Social Change:** Exposure to new worlds and new ideas can embolden people to challenge traditions at home.
- ❖ **Investment in Women Yields Generational Returns:** The impact of educating women compounds — in families, in communities, and across generations.

Reflect & Explore

1. **Generational Shifts:** Think about the women in your own ancestry. How did education — or the lack of it — shape their lives? What new doors opened for you that were closed for them?
2. **Challenging Norms:** Who in your life has dared to break with convention? What did their courage make possible for you or for others?
3. **The Power of Your Education:** How has your learning, formal or informal, changed your path? What are you doing to keep learning, and how can you use your knowledge to open doors for someone else?

As I carry this legacy forward, the next chapter asks: How do we make sure the ripples of change reach every girl, in every village, until no dream is out of reach and every generation rises higher than the last?

CHAPTER 26
Awakening the Giant Within

There's a moment in every life—sometimes quiet, sometimes seismic—where you catch a glimpse of the power inside you. Maybe it's a flash of confidence at the end of a hard-won project, or the steady certainty that comes from doing the right thing, even when it's hard. Often, it's fleeting. We return to our routines, our doubts and distractions, and the sense of something vast within us fades. But it never disappears. The giant within sleeps, waiting.

This chapter is about waking that giant—not just for ourselves, but for each other. It's about moving past fear, past the limits we've accepted, and helping others rise as we rise. Because potential, once released, is contagious. Empowerment multiplies. And when we build supportive ecosystems, we make space for everyone to flourish.

Purpose: The Engine That Drives Us

What gets you out of bed in the morning? Not just the alarm, not just the emails stacking up, but the reason behind it all. For years, I chased achievement—degrees, promotions, recognition—believing that if I just worked hard enough, I'd feel fulfilled. But the truth is, achievement without purpose feels hollow after a while. It's like running a race with no finish line.

Somewhere along the way, I started searching for something deeper. I wanted my work to matter, not just to me but to the people around me. I wanted to build things that lasted, to create spaces where people felt seen and valued. Words like grounded, confident, flow, and creativity became my new goals—states of being rather than boxes ticked off a list.

Purpose, I learned, is fuel. It's what keeps you going when the grind feels endless. And it's what gives you the courage to try something new, to speak up, to reach for more.

The Call to Humanize Work

For me, purpose crystallized around a simple idea: humanizing the workplace. I'd seen too many offices where collaboration was just a buzzword, where people competed more than they cooperated, where fear kept ideas small and voices silent. I wanted to help build something different—a place where people could bring their whole selves to work, where they felt safe to contribute, and where leadership meant lifting others up, not holding them down.

It's not easy. It requires patience, humility, and a willingness to sit with discomfort. But when you see a team move from guarded silence to genuine collaboration, when someone steps into their power and finds their voice, you realize how much is possible when you nurture rather than control.

The Spiritual and Societal Echo

This personal mission echoes something bigger—a spiritual and societal call to awaken potential. I've encountered phrases that stick in my mind: a "divine ordinance to produce spiritually enlightened, skillful, and hardworking youth across the world," or the charge to "ignite the minds for national development." We are reminded again and again that "our children are our future," and that, as Frederick Douglass said, "It is easier to build strong children than repair broken adults."

Potential in youth is immense. Even a single child, like Bhagwan Swaminarayan taught, "can change the entire history of humanity." But potential, no matter how vast, needs direction, encouragement, and the right environment to take root.

Vision: Seeing the Whole Elephant

Too often, we operate with fragmented perspectives, like the parable of the six blind men each touching a different part of the elephant and declaring they know the whole animal. Real progress requires vision—the ability to see the big picture, to connect the dots, and to recognize that everyone's piece of the puzzle matters.

Visionaries aren't just dreamers; they're builders. A country, a company, a family without vision is like a ship without a compass. We need people willing to look beyond their own experience, to ask hard questions, and to imagine what could be instead of settling for what is.

Wisdom in Simplicity

Some of the wisest leaders I've known—teachers, spiritual guides, even colleagues—have a gift for making complex things simple. Pramukh Swami Maharaj, for example, could convey deep truths using plain language and relatable stories. Dr. A.P.J. Abdul Kalam was famous for his "common sense" approach, cutting through jargon to what actually mattered.

We tend to overcomplicate things, especially when we're anxious or trying to prove ourselves. But often, the most profound truths are the simplest: treat people with respect; listen more than you speak; don't waste time being someone else. These aren't just platitudes—they're guideposts for unlocking potential in ourselves and others.

Unity in Diversity: Flourishing Together

Real progress—real peace—doesn't come from sameness. It comes from the ability to embrace diversity and still find common ground. In the workplace, in communities, in families, flourishing together means recognizing that we're stronger when we bring different perspectives, backgrounds, and strengths to the table.

Religious unity, spiritual purity, and cultural harmony are lofty ideals, but at their core, they're about respect—about seeing the humanity in one another. The secret of peace, as I've learned, is not in winning every argument but in building ecosystems where everyone can thrive.

The Courage to Be Yourself

There's a huge temptation, especially early in your career or when you're feeling insecure, to shape yourself into what you think others want. But every time you bend yourself to fit someone else's mold, you shrink your own potential. As Oscar Wilde put it, "Be yourself; everyone else is already taken."

Authenticity isn't just a buzzword—it's the foundation of real impact. When you bring your whole self to your work, you give others permission to do the same. You become a mirror, reflecting possibility, and a lamp, lighting the way.

Friction Polishes the Mirror

No one likes conflict, friction, or failure. But Rumi's question haunts me: "If you are irritated with every rub, how will your mirror be polished?" Growth never happens in comfort. Every challenge, every disagreement, every setback is a chance to learn, to reflect, and to refine who you are.

It's not about seeking out conflict for its own sake, but about reframing difficulties as opportunities. The leaders I most admire are the ones who respond to challenges with curiosity, not defensiveness. They ask, "What can I learn from this? How can I do better next time?"

Empowerment Multiplies

Here's where the magic happens: when you awaken your own potential, you automatically create space for others to awaken theirs. Empowerment is contagious. When you champion someone else—when you mentor, support, or simply believe in them—you start a ripple effect. They, in turn, do the same for others.

I've seen this most clearly in my work with women. When you help someone see their own strength, when you coach them through self-doubt and celebrate their wins, you don't just change one life—you change the whole ecosystem. Teams become more resilient. Organizations grow more adaptable. The culture shifts from scarcity to abundance.

Personal Story: Purpose, Potential, and the Path to Flourishing

If you'd asked me years ago what drove me, I might have pointed to career goals or financial security. But over time, those answers felt smaller and smaller compared to the questions that kept bubbling up:

- ❖ Who am I, beneath the titles and the to-do lists?
- ❖ What am I here to build?
- ❖ Whose lives do I touch, and how do I want them to remember me?

I found myself craving more than inspiration—I wanted transformation. I wanted to move past talking about empowerment and actually create it, for myself and for others.

My mission began to crystallize: I wanted to humanize the workplace, to build real teams where people felt safe and seen. I wanted to create environments where collaboration was more than a poster on the wall. I wanted to help people blossom, not just as workers but as human beings.

This wasn't just a personal revelation. It echoed the spiritual teachings I grew up with—the idea that each of us is born to blossom, to bring light, and to help others do the same. Whether you call it a "divine ordinance" or simply a responsibility to the next generation, the message is the same: awakening our potential is both a personal and a collective journey.

And so, I started small. I became more intentional about how I led, how I mentored, how I listened. I encouraged the people around me—especially women—to take risks, to speak up, to own their power. I celebrated their wins and helped them learn from their stumbles.

Over time, I watched the ecosystem change. Teams became stronger, more creative, more resilient. People started to believe in themselves—and each other. The giant within, once sleeping, began to wake.

Pearls of Insight

- ❖ **Purpose Fuels Action:** When you connect your work to a deeper purpose, you tap into a well of motivation and resilience that can sustain you through any challenge.
- ❖ **Nurture Potential:** Investing in people—especially youth, but also peers and colleagues—is the surest way to build a better future.
- ❖ **Simplicity Reveals Truth:** Don't overcomplicate things. The most powerful ideas are often the simplest, and the

most effective leaders know how to communicate them clearly.

- ❖ **Unity in Diversity:** Embrace differences. Seek to understand, not just to be understood. Build systems where everyone can flourish.
- ❖ **Authenticity is Power:** Bring your whole self, not just your work self. The more authentic you are, the more impact you'll have.
- ❖ **Friction Polishes:** Don't shy away from challenges. Use them to refine your skills, your values, and your vision.
- ❖ **Empowerment Multiplies:** When you help others realize their potential, you ignite a chain reaction of growth and positive change.

Your Turn: Reflect & Explore

1. **Your Core Purpose:** What drives you, beyond your job title or your paycheck? What legacy do you want to leave? Take time to write it down, revisit it often, and let it guide your choices.
2. **Nurturing Potential:** How do you help others grow? Maybe you mentor young people, support a colleague, or build community in your neighborhood. Look for new ways to invest in the potential around you.
3. **Embracing Friction:** Think back to a recent challenge. How did you respond? What did you learn? How could you reframe similar experiences in the future as opportunities for growth, rather than threats?

Building Ecosystems of Support

No one wakes the giant within alone. We need teachers, mentors, friends, and sometimes even critics. We need safe spaces to try, fail, and try again. We need cultures that value growth over perfection, learning over blame.

If you're in a position of influence—formal or informal—use it to build these ecosystems. Champion collaboration over competition. Celebrate vulnerability as much as victory. Make it safe to take risks, to ask for help, to be human.

The Giant is Already There

If you take one thing from this chapter, let it be this: your potential is bigger than your fear. It's there, waiting, even on days when you feel small or stuck or invisible. Don't waste time being someone else. The world needs what only you can offer.

And when you awaken your own giant, don't stop there. Look around. Who can you empower today? Whose inner light can you help ignite? The legacy of your life will be measured not just by what you achieve, but by how many others you help to rise.

Awaken the giant within. Then become the catalyst for others to do the same. Together, we build a world where everyone has room to blossom.

CHAPTER 27
Invisible to Invincible

Have you ever sat in a crowded room and felt like a ghost—speaking, but your words drift away unheard? Invisibility isn't always about being unseen; sometimes it's about being overlooked, underestimated, or mistaken for silence. But invisibility is not destiny. The journey from invisible to invincible begins with one bold decision: to step forward and claim your space, even when your voice shakes.

There's a moment—sometimes a flash, sometimes a slow dawning—when you realize the power inside you is vaster than you ever imagined. Maybe it's the surge of pride after a hard-won victory, or the quiet certainty that comes from standing your ground when it matters. Most days, that giant within us slumbers, lulled by routine and self-doubt. But it's always there, waiting for us to wake it up.

If you've ever sat in a crowded room and felt like a ghost, you know exactly what it means to be invisible. It's not always the kind of invisibility you can see in a mirror—it's deeper, quieter, and, sometimes, far more painful. Sometimes it's the sensation of speaking up and watching your words drift away, unacknowledged. Other times it's the ache of being overlooked, of having your effort mistaken for silence, your difference mistaken for insignificance.

Most of us, at some point, have lived on the edges—unseen, unheard, underestimated. But invisibility doesn't have to be our destiny. This chapter is about the journey from invisible to invincible: about making the choice, again and again, to step forward, to be seen, and to help others do the same. It's about claiming your space, your voice, your value—and turning that visibility into a platform for those still waiting in the shadows.

The Reluctant Spotlight: Leading from the Shadows for Those Still in Them

By nature, I'm shy. Not the cute, quirky kind of shy that's celebrated in movies, but the kind rooted in a deep, almost cellular insecurity. My comfort zone is the background. I'm the one quietly working, listening more than speaking, blending in rather than standing out. Big events? Networking mixers? Facilitating workshops? I can do them, sometimes even enjoy them in bursts, but they drain me. Afterward, I crave solitude—not because I'm antisocial, but because it's how I recalibrate. For introverts like me, solitude isn't a weakness. It's survival.

Still, life keeps nudging me into the light. Sometimes gently, sometimes with a shove. Early on, I tried to avoid it, clinging to the edges, hoping someone else would speak up, lead, or take the hit. But the world doesn't always allow bystanders. There are moments when you're the only one left who can say what needs to be said, or do what needs to be done. So, I started stepping up—not because I wanted to, but because the cause, the team, or the principle mattered more than my comfort.

Climbing the leadership ladder, building a more visible profile, comes with a constant hum of anxiety. "Why am I doing this?" my inner critic whispers. "Why not just sit back and coast? Why put myself out there, exposed and open to judgment?" The pressure to be "on" is real, and it's exhausting. But every time I consider retreating, I remember the barriers I've faced—the ones that made me invisible in the first place.

I remember what it felt like to be the only woman of color in the room. I remember the times I was talked over, passed up, or simply ignored. I remember carving my own path through systems that weren't built for someone like me. And I remember that my visibility isn't just about me. Every time I take up space, I do it for the women—especially women of color—still fighting for a seat at the table, for the chance to be heard and valued.

At a certain point, visibility stops being a personal choice and starts feeling like a responsibility. If my presence makes it a little easier for the next woman to speak up, if my success chips away at the bias that says leadership belongs to extroverts, then stepping forward is worth every ounce of discomfort. Introverted leaders bring deep thinking, careful observation, and empathy to the table. We lead not with volume, but with intentionality and presence. And the world desperately needs that.

Visibility Is a Choice—And a Practice

Let's clear up a myth: being seen isn't something that "just happens." Visibility is a choice, sometimes a daily one. It's the decision to speak up in a meeting, to share your work, to claim credit for your contributions. It's the courage to say, "I have something to offer," even when you're not sure anyone will listen.

But it's also a practice. No one is born invincible. You build that muscle by taking small risks, again and again, until standing in your power feels less like an act of rebellion and more like a natural part of who you are.

For me, visibility started in small ways—asking a question in a meeting, sharing my opinion on a team call, publishing my thoughts on LinkedIn. Each step was terrifying, but each one made the next a little easier. Over time, I realized that most people aren't waiting to judge me—they're just waiting to connect. Authenticity, even when messy, draws people in.

The Power of Representation

I didn't understand the true impact of visibility until women began reaching out to me. They'd say, "I follow your journey," or "I showed your story to my daughter." Some would confide that seeing someone who looked like them leading, building, and sometimes stumbling gave them hope. It made their dreams seem less far-fetched.

That's when it hit me: representation isn't a slogan. It's oxygen. When you see someone "like you" succeeding, it sneaks past your defenses and whispers, "Maybe you can do it, too." That's why it's so important for all of us—especially those from marginalized groups—to take up space, even when it's scary.

I have never forgotten my own role models: strong, purposeful women who led with quiet conviction. They weren't perfect, but they were real. Their stories gave me a map when my own world felt small and limiting. Now, I hope my journey is a small beacon for others. Not because I have it all figured out, but because I'm willing to keep trying, keep learning, and keep leading—even when the spotlight feels too bright.

Authentic Leadership: Embracing Imperfection

Let's be honest: leadership is messy. I run my own business, and I make mistakes all the time—some small, some spectacular. Early on, I tried to hide them, thinking that's what leaders do. But over time, I realized that pretending to have it all together is isolating, both for me and for those watching.

The truth is, people don't need flawless role models. They need real ones. They need to see that struggle is part of the story, that vulnerability and courage can co-exist. Sharing my mistakes, my doubts, and my learnings has built more trust and connection than any polished victory ever could.

And for introverts, this matters even more. The expectation to be "on" all the time is draining, sometimes paralyzing. But leading with authenticity—owning your quirks, your energy patterns, your need for downtime—models a healthier, more sustainable version of leadership. It gives others permission to do the same.

Purpose as Fuel

When the discomfort of visibility gets too loud, I return to my "why." It's never about the title, the applause, or the awards. It's about paving the way. Every barrier I break, every room I enter, every time I choose to be seen, I do it for those still waiting in the wings. I do it for the girls who will come after me, so maybe their journey will be a little smoother, their dreams a little closer.

Purpose is what keeps me moving when my energy is low or my confidence is shaken. It's what transforms anxiety into action, and action into influence. When you connect your visibility to something bigger than yourself, you find reserves of strength you never knew existed.

Echoes of Shakti: An Award, a Platform, a Promise

Recognition is a funny thing. When I received an award from my mother country, India, on International Women's Day, I was overwhelmed. The timing made it even more meaningful—it was Shivaratri, a festival honoring the creative power of the divine feminine. Standing in that room, surrounded by phenomenal women and their allies, I felt the energy of Naari Shakti—Woman Power—flowing through generations.

But here's what I know: the award wasn't just for me. It was for every woman who has ever been told to shrink, to hush, to wait her turn. It was for my ancestors, who toiled in the harsh lands of the Rann of Kutch, for those who risked everything to cross oceans, for my parents who broke barriers so I could have choices. Their sacrifices built the foundation I stand on. My recognition is their legacy, echoing forward.

Recognition, I've learned, isn't an endpoint. It's a platform. The true honor is not in receiving, but in what you do with it. My commitment is to use it to amplify the voices of women—especially women of color—still navigating the steepest climbs.

To advocate for diversity, inclusion, and equity, and to help create more seats at the table for those who have been excluded for too long.

Visibility as a Platform for Others

Being seen isn't just about personal validation. It's about making space for others. Every time you use your platform—whether it's a job title, a social media account, a seat in the boardroom—you have the chance to help someone else be seen. That could mean calling out bias, sharing credit, mentoring someone new, or simply listening to a story that would otherwise go unheard.

The most powerful leaders I know aren't the loudest in the room; they're the ones who make space for others to shine. They use their visibility as a shield for the vulnerable, a microphone for the unheard, a door for the excluded.

The Strength of Quiet Influence

There's a story we've all been sold: that leadership looks like charisma, extroversion, a booming voice, and a fearless presence. But leadership comes in many forms. Quiet influence—the ability to listen, reflect, empathize, and respond thoughtfully—is one of the most powerful, and often the most overlooked.

Introverts, in particular, bring gifts that are desperately needed: deep focus, measured decision-making, and the ability to see nuances others might miss. Our culture often equates extroversion with capability, but it's a bias that needs challenging. Some of the most effective, transformative leaders move quietly, but their impact is thunderous.

Rest and Recovery: Honoring Your Energy

Visibility doesn't mean burning out in the name of exposure. For introverts, managing energy is crucial. After a major event or a day spent "on stage," I've learned to schedule downtime—time to recharge, reflect, and just be. This isn't selfish; it's smart. It allows me to return to my work with clarity and renewed purpose. It also sets an example for others: your value isn't measured by your ability to be "on" 24/7.

Recognition as a Platform, Not a Finish Line

Awards and public recognition feel great, but they're not the end goal. They're a tool—a way to open doors, start conversations, and support others. The true measure of success is how you use your platform to make things better for those who come after you.

When I held that award, I thought of the women who would never be recognized publicly for their Labour, their courage, their perseverance. My job is to honour them by paying it forward—by opening doors, advocating for change, and reminding others that their stories matter.

The Power of Legacy

Every achievement rests on the foundation laid by those before us. My ancestors, literal and figurative, shaped my path. Their struggles, hopes, and sacrifices are woven into every step I take. Acknowledging their impact grounds me. It reminds me that my success isn't just mine. It's a continuation of a story that began long before I was born—and one that will continue long after I'm gone.

Legacy isn't about statues or headlines. It's about the lives you touch, the opportunities you create, the courage you inspire. It's about making sure that when you become visible, you leave the door open for others to follow.

Your potential is bigger than your fear. Awaken your giant, and then look around: who else can you empower? The true legacy of your life is not just in what you achieve, but in how many others you help to rise. The world needs what only you can offer—so rise, and help others rise with you.

Legacy isn't measured by headlines or awards, but by the lives you touch and the doors you open for others. When you choose to be visible, you become proof for someone else that their dreams are possible too. Rise—and help others rise with you

Pearls of Insight

- ❖ **Visibility is a Choice and a Practice:** You decide, every day, whether to step up and be seen. It gets easier with practice, but it's always an act of courage.
- ❖ **Introversion is Not a Barrier to Leadership:** Some of the best leaders are quiet, thoughtful, and deeply empathetic. Don't let anyone tell you otherwise.
- ❖ **Purpose Fuels Persistence:** When you connect your efforts to something bigger than yourself, you find the strength to keep going—even when it's hard.
- ❖ **Recognition as a Platform:** Use every bit of visibility you gain to amplify others, advocate for change, and further your mission.
- ❖ **Authenticity Over Perfection:** People need real role models, not flawless ones. Share your struggles as well as your successes.
- ❖ **Representation Matters:** When you're visible, you become proof for others that their dreams are possible, too.
- ❖ **Manage Your Energy:** Know your limits and honor your need for rest. You serve no one by running on empty.
- ❖ **Paying It Forward:** The ultimate goal of visibility is to make the path easier for those who come next.

Your Turn: Reflect & Explore

1. **When Have You Felt Invisible?** Think back to a time when you felt overlooked or unheard. What did you need in that moment? Who, if anyone, helped you feel seen again?
2. **How Can You Help Others Be Seen?** What small action can you take today to lift someone else out of invisibility? Maybe it's giving credit, amplifying a quiet voice, or simply listening without judgment.
3. **Your Energy Source:** Do you gain energy from people and activity, or do you recharge in solitude? How can you design your work and leadership style to fit your natural rhythm?
4. **Stepping Out of Comfort:** Recall a time you had to do something public or visible that made you uneasy. What pushed you forward? What did you learn?
5. **Your "Why":** Beyond ambition or obligation, what deeper purpose could fuel your willingness to be visible, to lead, to take up space?
6. **Your Foundation:** Who paved the way for you—mentors, family, ancestors? How does their story shape your own sense of responsibility and gratitude?
7. **Using Your Platform:** What platforms—formal or informal—do you have right now? How could you use one to advocate for a cause, support others, or amplify an unheard voice?
8. **Paying It Forward:** What's one concrete action you can take this month to support someone else's journey? A recommendation, a public thank you, an introduction, or a simple note of encouragement?

As we each move from the shadows to the spotlight, the next chapter asks: how do we create a world where everyone's story is seen, valued, and empowered to shape the future?

CHAPTER 28
Unboxed—Your Turn to Lead

Take a breath—the kind that settles your bones and says, "I made it." You've walked through stories, wrestled with questions, and felt the tug of possibility. This isn't just the end of a book; it's the moment you step out of the box others built for you. What if you stopped waiting for permission and started leading on your own terms, right now?

This chapter is an invitation. Not to be perfect, or fearless, or finished. But to step forward. Unboxed. Unapologetic. Ready to lead on your own terms.

The Power of Beginning Again

Let's start with a truth that should be stitched into every handbook, every leadership manual, every whispered piece of advice passed between friends: You are allowed to change. You are allowed to begin again. You are allowed to lead.

Somewhere along the way, we get boxed in—by other people's expectations, our own self-doubt, the roles that feel too small or too safe. We start to believe that who we are is fixed, etched in stone. But the truth is, you can reinvent yourself at any moment. You can choose a new direction, claim a new voice, start again—right now.

The world is full of people who will try to define you by your past, your mistakes, your quietness, your difference. Let them talk. You know better. You know you are a work in progress—a story still being written. And every page is yours to shape.

Your Story Matters

Here's something I wish someone had told me long before I learned it the hard way: Your story matters. Not because it's dramatic, or tidy, or fits into a neat narrative arc. But because it is yours. Because it holds truths that no one else can tell. Because the act of telling it—of standing in your own experience, your own worth—is a kind of leadership the world desperately needs.

You don't have to be the loudest voice in the room to change the conversation. Sometimes, the most powerful thing you can do is speak your story, just as it is. To say: "This is how I got here. This is what I learned. This is what I still don't know." That kind of honesty is electric. It draws people in. It builds bridges where there were once walls.

When My Power Meets Yours: Embracing Worth, Unleashing Voice

Recently, in a quiet moment, a phrase landed in my mind like a stone dropped in water: Don't diminish your worth. At first glance, it seemed almost trite. But as the ripples spread, I realized how much of my life had been shaped by the habit of shrinking, of holding back, of playing small to fit into rooms not meant for me.

As a woman of color, just getting in—securing a seat at the table—felt like the victory. Once there, it was all about not rocking the boat, not drawing too much attention, not giving anyone a reason to regret letting me in. It's a survival tactic, born of scarcity. But it's also a trap. You end up stifling the very qualities that make you valuable. You start to believe that safety lies in conformity, even as, deep down, you know: "The reward for conformity is that everyone likes you but yourself." (Rita Mae Brown said it best.)

Then came the wake-up call. As a mother to two daughters, I had to ask: What am I role modelling? If I make myself small, if I teach by example that playing it safe is the best way to survive, what am I passing on? That realization terrified me more than any risk I could ever take.

Around that time, I heard a message—echoed in leadership programs and in the voices of women who'd walked this road before me: You've worked hard. You've earned your seat. You've delivered impact. Now use your voice for the greater good. This isn't arrogance. It's responsibility. It's the understanding that playing small does not serve the world.

Why do we fear our own power? Maybe because it's easier to stay invisible, to keep the peace, to avoid the discomfort of standing out. Maybe because we're taught that humility means hiding our light. But real humility is knowing your worth and using it to lift others. It's recognizing that when you stand in your power, you're not a threat—you're an invitation. Collaboration, not competition. Celebration, not insecurity. Abundance, not scarcity.

When I finally internalized this—that I didn't need to shrink for anyone else to shine—it was terrifying. But it was also freeing. I could be visible. I could speak. I could lead, not because I was perfect, but because I was ready to be real.

Unboxed: The Invitation

So here it is—your invitation to step forward, unboxed. To claim your seat. To use your voice. To rewrite the story, for yourself and for those watching.

Don't wait for someone else to give you permission. Don't wait for the moment when you finally feel "ready" (it may never come). Don't wait for the world to change before you show up. Show up, and let the world change around you.

There will always be people who want to put you back in your box. Who will tell you to be smaller, quieter, safer. But you know better now. You have seen your own strength, your own resilience, your own capacity for courage. You have a responsibility to use it—not just for yourself, but for all those who need to see what's possible.

You don't need to be flawless or fearless to lead. You only need to be willing—to show up, to speak your truth, to claim your space. Every time you do, you give others permission to do the same. The world is waiting. Your turn.

Pearls of Insight

- ❖ **Acknowledge Your Worth:** You are enough, right now. Your value is not up for debate, not contingent on anyone else's approval. It's grounded in your skills, your story, your impact.
- ❖ **Playing Small is a Disservice:** The world needs your full voice, your boldest ideas, your authentic self. Holding back serves no one—not you, not those watching you, not the future you want to build.
- ❖ **Authenticity Requires Courage:** Being true to yourself, especially when it goes against the grain, is the bravest thing you can do. It's also the most magnetic.
- ❖ **Earned Place, Earned Voice:** You've proven yourself. Now use your position to advocate, to amplify, to speak for those who can't yet speak for themselves.
- ❖ **Empowered People Empower Others:** When you stand in your own power, you free others to do the same. You become a living, breathing invitation for others to rise.

Workbook: Reflect & Explore

If you're ready, grab a notebook, a pen, the back of an envelope—anything to catch your thoughts. This is your space to dream, to plan, to commit. There are no right answers, only honest ones.

1. What's Your Next Brave Step?

Think about the area of your life where you feel the urge to move, to stretch, to risk. Maybe it's speaking up at work, setting a new boundary, applying for a role that feels out of reach, starting something of your own, or saying yes to an opportunity that scares you a little.

- ❖ What does that next step look like?
- ❖ What would it mean to take it?
- ❖ What's holding you back?
- ❖ Write it out. Be as specific as you can.

2. What Legacy Do You Want to Leave?

Fast-forward to a future where your work, your presence, your story has made a mark.

- ❖ What do you want people to remember about you?
- ❖ What impact do you want to have on your family, your community, your field?
- ❖ What values do you want to be known for?

Let yourself dream big. Your legacy isn't just about grand achievements—it's about the ripples you create in every interaction, every choice.

3. Diminishing Habits

Be honest: In what ways do you still play small, hold back, or diminish your worth?

- ❖ When do you notice yourself shrinking?
- ❖ What triggers it—fear, criticism, habit?
- ❖ What would it look like to stop?

Bring these habits into the light. Awareness is the first step to change.

4. Owning Your Seat

Reflect on the evidence that you belong where you are.

- ❖ List your achievements, big and small.
- ❖ Recall moments when you made a difference.
- ❖ Gather the feedback, the thank-yous, the wins.

Let this list be your reminder the next time imposter syndrome comes knocking.

5. Using Your Voice

This week, commit to one situation where you'll use your voice more fully.

- ❖ What's the scenario?
- ❖ What's the message you want to share?
- ❖ What's the smallest step you can take to speak more authentically?

Remember: Every time you use your voice, you give permission to someone else to use theirs.

You Are Allowed

You are allowed to change your mind. To grow. To outgrow. To make mistakes. To begin again. To lead.

You are allowed to say, "I want more." You are allowed to want different. You are allowed to want better—for yourself, for your children, for your community.

You are allowed to take up space. To be seen. To be heard. To be unboxed.

Final Reflections: The Journey Continues

If you've been waiting for a sign that it's time to step forward, this is it. If you've been waiting for permission, consider it granted. If you've been waiting for someone to say, "Your story matters," hear it now—loud and clear.

Leadership isn't a title, or a destination, or a set of bullet points on a resume. It's a way of moving through the world. It's the quiet choices, the brave stands, the moments when you choose honesty over comfort, growth over safety, possibility over fear.

You don't have to have all the answers. You don't have to be fearless, or flawless, or finished. You just have to be willing. Willing to show up, to listen, to learn, to lead.

And when you do—when you step forward, unboxed, and claim your voice—you give others permission to do the same. You change the story, not just for yourself, but for everyone watching.

So what's your next brave step? What legacy will you leave? The world is waiting. Your turn.

You've walked the road from invisible to invincible. Now, the box is open. The path is yours. Step forward. Unboxed. Lead on.

There is no next chapter written for you—only the blank page ahead. The story continues with every brave step you take. Lead on, unboxed.

Epilogue

What if every ending is just a disguised beginning? If you've made it here, thank you for walking alongside me—whether in a single breathless sitting or over months of busy days. Your presence on this journey means more than you know.

None of us are finished stories. I used to think the point of life was to find the neat ending—the job, the relationship, the version of myself I could finally settle into. But every time I thought I'd arrived, life handed me a twist or a left turn. The moments that looked like endings—the job loss, the heartbreak, the move, the uncertain leap—were usually beginnings in disguise. The universe, it turns out, is a master at rerouting us toward growth.

For years, I saw certain parts of myself as flaws to be corrected or outgrown. Curiosity made me restless. Restlessness felt like a lack of gratitude. Hope sometimes felt naïve. But over time, I realized these weren't burdens—they were lifelines. Curiosity kept me learning, asking questions, refusing to settle for "just because." Restlessness nudged me out of comfort zones and into new worlds. Hope gave me the courage to begin again, even when I had no guarantees.

If there's one truth I hope you carry with you, it's this: You are allowed to change. You can start over as many times as you need. There is no expiration date on transformation. The version of you that exists today is not the final draft. You can rewrite your story as often as your heart asks for it. Sometimes it's a big, sweeping change; sometimes it's a quiet decision to try again. Both count. Both matter.

We spend so much of our lives seeking permission—permission to speak, to want more, to leave, to stay, to try again after we fail. Let this be your permission slip, in case you need it. You don't have to wait for someone else to tell you it's okay to begin again, or to become something new. The world needs your story—messy chapters, plot twists, unfinished sentences and all.

Your story matters—not because it's perfect or dramatic, but because it's yours. Every messy chapter, every plot twist, every unfinished sentence is proof that you are still becoming. If you ever doubt your voice, remember: the act of owning your story is more than enough. It sends ripples into the world you may never see.

So thank you for sharing this path. For every time you risked a new beginning, every time you chose hope over resignation, every time you reminded yourself that you are allowed to change—thank you. Keep going. **The best stories are the ones still being written.**

Resources & Next Steps

This is not the end—it's a launching pad. The real transformation happens in the quiet, everyday choices you make from here on out. If you're wondering how to keep the momentum alive, here are some resources and next steps to support your journey.

Reflection Prompts

Start with the "Your Turn" questions from each chapter. Don't just read them—write your answers down. Journal honestly, even if you don't know the answers yet. Revisit your responses every few months. You'll be surprised by how your perspective shifts as you grow. These prompts become a mirror, showing you just how far you've come and reminding you where you still want to go.

Daily Practices

Change doesn't come from grand gestures—it's built on tiny, consistent acts. Try a morning check-in: before the day gets noisy, ask yourself, "What do I need today?" In the evening, pause and reflect: "What am I proud of? What do I want to carry forward?" A weekly review—ten quiet minutes to look back and look ahead—can help you course-correct and celebrate progress. These rituals anchor you in your intentions, especially when life gets busy.

Building Your Circle

You don't have to do this alone. Seek out mentors, friends, or a book club that aligns with your values. Find people who challenge and champion you, who listen without judgment and push you to be your best. If you can't find them nearby, look online—there are communities everywhere, waiting for you to show up as you are. Remember: leadership is a team sport. Let yourself be supported, and offer your support in return.

Professional Support

Sometimes, the bravest thing you can do is ask for help. If you're feeling stuck, overwhelmed, or just need an objective perspective, consider working with a therapist, coach, or counselor. Professional support isn't a sign of weakness—it's an investment in your wellbeing and growth.

Giving Back

As you rise, lift others. Mentor someone coming up behind you. Volunteer in your community. Share your story. The impact you make ripples outward, often in ways you'll never see. Giving back isn't just about charity—it's about building the kind of world you want to live in.

Permission Slips

Write yourself permission slips as often as you need: permission to rest, to say no, to play, to hope, to start over. Stick them in your notebook, on your fridge, or in your phone. Let them remind you that you don't need anyone else's approval to honor your needs and dreams.

This is your next chapter. Keep it honest. Keep it brave. You've got this.

Conclusion

The journey isn't neat, and it's never really done. What matters isn't how perfectly you follow the "rules," but how bravely you write your own. The powers you need—curiosity, hope, rest, play, kindness, generosity, perspective, faith, and the courage to say no—are already within you.

This book is my offering, but the next chapters belong to you. Go write them bravely

About the Author

Premila Jina knows what it means to feel boxed in and underestimated—especially as a woman of colour—and what it takes to break free. Born in India, raised in Kenya, shaped by years in London's high-pressure finance world, and now calling Perth home, she's walked the long road from invisible to invincible. For years, Premila tried to fit into spaces that didn't see her, playing small just to survive. She's learned firsthand the cost of silence—and the power of finding your voice as a woman of colour.

This book is her lived invitation to **women of colour**, and anyone tired of shrinking or waiting for permission to lead. Through honest stories, practical prompts, and hard-won wisdom, Premila challenges you to rewrite your script and show up whole—at work, at home, in the world. Her journey, marked by missteps, fresh starts, and a refusal to settle, is proof that real leadership starts from the inside out.

Premila believes the world needs more voices, not fewer—especially from women of colour. We need more leaders willing to be unboxed and unapologetically themselves. If you're ready to stop playing small and start leading with authenticity, consider this your sign: **your story matters, your voice is needed, and the time to lead is now**.

The Rise and Radiate Program: From Unwritten to Unleashed

From Pages to Purpose: The Journey Beyond "The Unwritten Leader"

As you close this final chapter of "The Unwritten Leader," you've journeyed through stories of resilience, witnessed the power of authentic leadership, and perhaps recognized your own experiences reflected in these pages. The research, insights, and lived experiences shared throughout this book have illuminated a profound truth: women of colour possess extraordinary leadership potential that remains largely untapped and unsupported in traditional spaces.

But awareness alone isn't enough. Recognition without action is simply another form of silence.

This realization sparked the creation of the Rise and Radiate Program—a direct response to the gap between knowing and doing, between understanding the challenges and actively dismantling them. Every story shared in this book, every statistic cited, every barrier identified has contributed to designing a comprehensive leadership empowerment program specifically for women of colour.

The Inspiration: When Stories Become Solutions

"Women of colour in Australian Workplaces" 2024 revealed that 68.4% of women of colour in Australia experience workplace discrimination, with racism accounting for 93.8% of these cases. These aren't just numbers—they represent our mothers, sisters, daughters, and colleagues whose talents remain unrecognized, whose voices remain unheard, and whose leadership potential remains unrealized.

The book's central thesis—that women of colour are "unwritten leaders" whose stories and contributions have been systematically erased or minimized—demanded more than documentation. It demanded action. It demanded a program that would help these unwritten leaders finally write their own stories of success, influence, and impact.

The Rise and Radiate Program: Turning Insights into Impact

Born from the research, stories, and frameworks explored throughout "The Unwritten Leader," the Rise and Radiate Program is a comprehensive 12-month leadership development journey specifically designed for women of colour. It transforms the book's insights into practical, life-changing experiences.

Program Foundation: The VOICE Framework™

Drawing directly from the leadership challenges identified in earlier chapters, the program centers on the VOICE Framework™—a five-pillar system that guides participants from feeling silenced to being seen, heard, valued, and respected:

V - Visibility & Values

- ❖ Clarify your unique identity and intersectional experiences
- ❖ Build an authentic personal brand that commands respect
- ❖ Develop executive presence that reflects your true worth
- ❖ Master the art of strategic visibility in professional spaces

O - Ownership & Authenticity

- ❖ Own your narrative and rewrite limiting beliefs
- ❖ Cultivate unshakeable confidence in your abilities and achievements
- ❖ Embrace your cultural heritage as a leadership strength
- ❖ Develop authentic leadership style that honours your identity

I - Influence & Impact

- ❖ Master assertive communication techniques
- ❖ Excel in public speaking and presentation skills
- ❖ Learn to express needs and boundaries with clarity and power
- ❖ Develop skills to influence decision-makers and drive change

C - Community & Courage

- ❖ Build supportive professional networks
- ❖ Navigate microaggressions with strategic responses
- ❖ Foster courage to advocate for yourself and others
- ❖ Create accountability partnerships for sustained growth

E - Empowerment & Excellence

- ❖ Sustain leadership growth through advanced skills development
- ❖ Become an advocate for systemic change
- ❖ Build resilience for long-term success
- ❖ Mentor and sponsor other women of colour

Program Structure: 12 Months of Transformation

Phase 1: Foundation (Months 1-3)

- ❖ **Full-Day Workshop 1:** "Finding Your Voice" - Identity, values, and authentic leadership
- ❖ Monthly individual coaching sessions
- ❖ Professional branding photoshoot and LinkedIn optimization
- ❖ Introduction to closed community platform

Phase 2: Development (Months 4-6)

- ❖ **Full-Day Workshop 2:** "Owning Your Power" - Confidence, communication, and influence
- ❖ Advanced presentation skills training
- ❖ Guest speaker series featuring successful women of colour leaders
- ❖ Peer mentoring circles and accountability partnerships

Phase 3: Application (Months 7-9)

- ❖ **Full-Day Workshop 3:** "Building Your Tribe" - Networking, community building, and strategic relationships

- Real-world leadership project with coaching support
- Microaggression response training and boundary-setting workshops
- Industry-specific networking events and introductions

Phase 4: Amplification (Months 10-12)

- **Full-Day Workshop 4:** "Radiating Your Impact" - Sustainable growth and paying it forward
- Capstone presentation showcasing leadership journey
- Graduation celebration and certification ceremony
- Alumni network integration and ongoing community access

Program Components: Comprehensive Support System

Individual Executive Coaching

- Monthly 90-minute one-on-one sessions
- Personalized action plans and goal setting
- Career advancement strategy development
- Confidential space for addressing specific challenges

Professional Branding Package

- Professional headshots and brand photography
- LinkedIn profile optimization
- Personal website development
- Media training for interviews and speaking opportunities

Exclusive Community Platform

- ❖ Private online space for 24/7 peer support
- ❖ Resource library with templates, guides, and tools
- ❖ Monthly virtual networking events
- ❖ Mentorship matching with program alumni

Expert Guest Faculty

- ❖ Successful women of colour in C-suite positions
- ❖ Entrepreneurs who've built multi-million dollar businesses
- ❖ Board directors and community leaders
- ❖ Industry experts in finance, technology, healthcare, and more

Skills Development Workshops

- ❖ Negotiation and salary advancement techniques
- ❖ Board readiness and governance training
- ❖ Public speaking and media presence
- ❖ Financial literacy and investment strategies

Who Should Join

The Rise and Radiate Program is designed for women of colour who:

- ❖ Hold or aspire to leadership positions in their organizations
- ❖ Feel ready to invest in their personal and professional development
- ❖ Want to build authentic networks with like-minded women
- ❖ Are committed to not just rising themselves, but lifting others as they climb

- ❖ Seek a safe space to discuss challenges unique to their intersectional identities
- ❖ Want to transform from being "unwritten leaders" to powerful, visible changemakers

Your Call to Action: Write Your Next Chapter

"The Unwritten Leader" has documented the challenges, celebrated the resilience, and illuminated the path forward. Now it's time to walk that path. The Rise and Radiate Program is your opportunity to move from reading about change to being the change.

This is more than a professional development program—it's a movement to ensure that no woman of colour remains an "unwritten leader." It's your chance to join a community of women who understand your journey, support your growth, and celebrate your success.

Connect with us on LinkedIn to learn more about our next cohort and secure your place in this transformative journey. Limited spots ensure intimate group sizes and personalized attention.

Your leadership story is waiting to be written. Let's write it together

Ready to rise and radiate? Connect with us on LinkedIn and join our tribe of women who are rewriting the leadership narrative, one voice at a time.

www.ingramcontent.com/pod-product-compliance
Lightning Source LLC
Chambersburg PA
CBHW022203090526
44583CB00012BA/277